The Library of Scandinavian Literature

CONTEMPORARY DANISH POETRY

Contemporary Danish Poetry

AN ANTHOLOGY

Edited by Line Jensen, Erik Vagn Jensen,
Knud Mogensen, Alexander D. Taylor

Introduction by Torben Brostrøm

TWAYNE PUBLISHERS
BOSTON, MASSACHUSETTS, U.S.A.

The Library of Scandinavian Literature
Erik J. Friis, *General Editor*

Volume 31

Contemporary Danish Poetry: An Anthology

This volume published under the auspices of the
Danish Ministry of Cultural Affairs.

Library of Congress Cataloging in Publication Data

Main entry under title:

Contemporary Danish poetry.

(The Library of Scandinavian literature ; v. 31)
(Twayne's international studies and translations ; TISAT 31)
1. Danish poetry—20th century.   I.   Jensen,
Line.   II.   Series.
PT 7978.C6   839.8'1'17408   77-2567
ISBN 0–8057–8157–9

Contents

Contents

Contents

Contents

Contents

Contents

Editors' Note

The purpose of this anthology is to show the English-speaking world a small corner of living Danish literature. Assisted by enthusiastic translators and after many personal discussions with most of them, we have tried to present, within the compass of an ordinary book, our personal choice of forty-seven Danish poets.

It is our hope that critics of this anthology will realize the difficulties of such a task and remember that poetry is often almost impossible to transfer from one culture and one language to another without loss of essential values.

In order to give an impression of what is happening and has happened, especially during the last twenty-five years, it has seemed natural to include also a few characteristic examples of some of the great poets from the beginning of the century and the interwar period.

In some instances we have found it reasonable to try to illustrate an author's development over a period of years—in other instances we have felt that the best way to bring out the distinctive character and tone of an author was to concentrate on some of his recent poems.

While preparing this anthology each of us has had many useful discussions with authors and translators and have received invaluable advice from all those who were interested in making the book as fine as possible. We are especially indebted to Poul Borum, the Danish poet and translator, for enthusiastic practical assistance. And to his American colleague, W. S. Merwin, for hundreds of ideas to improve the translations. His discussions with us as well as with fifteen of the authors represented here have been of great importance.

LINE JENSEN, ERIK VAGN JENSEN,
KNUD MOGENSEN, ALEXANDER D. TAYLOR

May, 1975

Introduction

By TORBEN BROSTRØM

For a description of modern Danish poetry, various historical points of departure may be chosen, e.g., the nearly century-old Naturalism with its new idea of man, coinciding with the emergence of industrialism and capitalism. In many respects we are still living under similar conditions, and poetry still finds answers to the challenges they present. The language of Naturalism, however, was not primarily that of lyric poetry. The age of modern poetry was heralded in the 1890s by the so-called Symbolists, and their major figure in this respect, Sophus Claussen, has been chosen as the introductory poet of this anthology. His knowledge of the fragmentation of consciousness, which is a characteristic feature of Modernism, was comprehensive, and in several ways modern Danish poetry has been determined by his striving to subdue and yet artistically preserve that fragmentation. This selection can but suggest some of his ways toward creating a poetic cognition, a synthesis superior to that of scientific, rational knowledge. That was his Heroica. In the final words of one of his poems: "draw ... final thoughts, filled with the motion of the Infinite." The novel element in the language of Symbolism and, hence, of Modernism is seen in his erotic poems where soul and landscape, I and thou, connect in personal, individual symbolic images. The unconscious becomes a new conscious domain for the poet. Here—and in nature as well—are the resources which are invoked to keep together a universe threatened by fragmentation.

This tension between opposing forces was not relaxed at the turn of the century or at the time of the First World War. Time and again it reappears in different shapes, but it becomes increasingly difficult to maintain the idealistic superstructure even though it is attempted through new linguistic experiments. While the geographical and political world is expanding and the means of communication are intensified, reality keeps presenting itself as an urgent problem, and almost everywhere in the Western world modernity is experienced as an internal disruption. Poetry is a series of attempts at subjective interpretation, and, in principle, the Danish answers to such challenges correspond to reactions found in other European countries. In the period before the Second World War the Danish responses were somewhat more restrained than those in Germany, France, and England, whereas after the war they were expressed in vehemently experimental forms, i.e. under the influence of European Modernism which now really established a tradition.

The survey of modern Danish poetry in this book includes the recent years in which the poetic activity has been exceptionally intense and virtually all kinds of poetry have been written. With e.g. Dan Turèll one finds an expansive kind of poetry which assimilates almost any kind of language: the poetry of the period after the youth revolt, perhaps inspired by the enthusiastic life of beat-lyrics and by their expansion of consciousness. The components of Turèll's language may have widely different origins. The poet speaks a searching language liberated from *style* in the sense of personal coloring. It characterizes an open, productive attitude, a constant creation with new formulations and conscious use of patterns and models. Among his contemporaries one also sees this gesture of liberation from a society like the Danish which has long been fixed by bourgeois standards. Poetry is no longer a religion, rather a matter of politics, a way of speaking about things.

Another retrospect. The other introductory figure of twentieth-century Danish poetry, Johannes V. Jensen, turned with all his will, though not always with all his being, against the spirit of decadence, doubt, and fragmentation. Instead he declared himself a man of facts in the manner of Walt Whitman, whose poems he translated into Danish. However, it is evident in Jensen's "At Memphis Station" that he did not accept wholeheartedly the new world with its noisy technology, machines, and advertising which, otherwise, he praised fervently in articles and reportages. The poem records the uneasiness of the heart which is symbolized by the journey. The impatience is also a symptom of that spirit of restlessness which is inherent in the conditions of production. The poet is fascinated by the technology of a locomotive: "Look how the engine, / that mighty machine, stands there calmly seething, / wrapping itself in smoke—it is patient." Whatever else, it is mundane, it has severed any connection with God, and to do so is the poet's aspiration as well. But he does not want to remain in one of the "poster-howling buildings" whose American way of life may conceal happiness. The great engine is chuffing and snorting, preparing for the journey through the desolate, but also fertile and in-spiring countryside of the fin-de-siècle mood—here the soul-corroding rain and the wet forests of the Mississippi.

There are several reasons for Johannes V. Jensen's acceptance of the industrialized, Anglo-American world—halfhearted though it is—among them a necessary approval of progress. But after the First World War Denmark was flooded by the entire mercantile advertisement world of capitalism. It was welcomed by Otto Gelsted in his poem "The Show Boat." With its leveling of all values and its reification of all human relations, it is a world of sensations entering the twilight harbor of Denmark. In a poetic-prose form, modeled after Johannes V. Jensen, Gelsted dissociated himself from everything his idol had staked on in his youth. What, indeed, is not on board?

> Here are clinics for make-up and bureaus for suicide,
> which men in despair can consult for a suitable fee;
> here are displayed the latest stunts of the doctor's art,
> men changed into women and women into men;
> here is the ship herself with all that's in vogue:
> tennis courts and swimming pools, the church and the
> newspaper office
> (that prints you the whole Bible in installments);
> here is the giant gyroscope,

    whose 180,000 revolutions to the minute
    neutralize all motion
    and safeguard the passengers from seasickness.

Gelsted organized his own youth revolt in the shape of a revolu-
tionary student sitting in a shanty with his finger on the button,
ready to blow up the entire masquerade of capitalism. A crash
is heard—but it did not re-echo in the world of reality which
remained problematic.

The outrage of Gelsted's revolutionary dream becomes a gen-
eral dream of catastrophe in Tom Kristensen's poem "Fear."
Originally, it is from his novel *Havoc*, which depicts the expe-
rience of total emptiness, of fear which can be resolved only
by the catastrophe. "I have longed for the final disaster / for
havoc and violent death." That was the result of the expressionist
worship of the chaotic beauty of modernity. The shapeless fear
had been scrutinized by Søren Kierkegaard, but now it marks
an era and can be found in various versions in Kafka, Heming-
way, and T. S. Eliot, to mention only a few examples. Expres-
sionism in Denmark was not excessive and pathetic as in
Germany; with great precision it annulled traditional values. It
was colorful and imaginative, and it was based on senses rather
than ideas, as may be seen in Tom Kristensen's poem "The
Execution," an extreme expression of confrontation with the
absurdity of death. From new points of departure, such con-
frontations became frequent in the second phase of Modernism,
the period after the Second World War.

If one compares "The Show Boat" by Gelsted and Tom Kris-
tensen's poems with respect to their description of life, it will
be seen that the former poem aims at objectivity in the sense
of relating to socioeconomic realities, whereas Tom Kristensen
is emphatically subjective. With him the world is a projection
of emotional states. Until recently, the most significant Danish
poems were written along these lines. The poets of the twenties
and thirties contributed little to the social analysis carried out
by a number of critical *prose* writers. As an example, one may

mention Jens August Schade. Through all the years his poetry has been a series of surprising expressions of the meeting of souls in the thoroughly sexualized universe he has created, made up of heavenly and human bodies, of Danish landscapes and townscapes. Without really being influenced by Surrealism, his poetry constitutes a clear parallel to it in its free motion between large and small, conscious and unconscious elements, meaningful coincidences which, with the certainty of the instinct, become regularities in a liberated view of the world. By means of libido, Schade has managed to ward off the fragmentation.

The poetry of the younger Gustaf Munch-Petersen is akin to Schade's, but as a consequence of the liberation of instincts Munch-Petersen strove for a political engagement; it must be used in a revolutionary manner. During his brief productive period he managed to express essential experiences of modernism, in both human and linguistic terms. The land below, which he describes in a poem with that title, is both the liberated collective subconscious and the natural socialism of the proletariat. In the last phase of his production, the universal and, hence, abstract I became identical with the personal I in such a way that the poem became a confession and an obligation to act. In consequence of this he went to Spain and took part in the struggle against Franco in the civil war. It cost him his life. Poetry and action became one.

The Symbolist poem ranks as a linguistic act of intrinsic value. In Danish poetry this tradition was continued most overtly by Paul la Cour, especially in his postwar poems. The poems are those very moments in which inspiration pervades the expectant consciousness and the unity of all things is established. In a series of theoretical reflections, "Fragments of a Diary," he professed his views on poetry as a general concept of existence, as that which collects the fragments and reveals the untraceable connections between all that is living. Thorkild Bjørnvig reacted against this identificational view of nature and man. The object should be maintained, the borders between subject and object must be respected if a true sense of com-

munity is to be experienced. Both poets are modern, are con-
noisseurs of chaos and fragmentation, but regardless of their
similarities, their interpretations are based on different philo-
sophical principles. However, the objective world of which
Bjørnvig speaks is still nature, rather than society, though in
a series of portrait-poems he has analyzed the titanic struggle of
the artist to maintain the world as is seen in e.g. Edgar Allan
Poe. Bjørnvig has launched yet another shipwreck in Danish
poetry, viz. "The Ballad of the 'Great Eastern,'" another de-
scription of the modernist concept of insanity, a ship of fools,
a ship of death which must be scrapped.

Bjørnvig belongs to the generation of poets that appeared
during the forties. They were characterized by the ideological
readjustments and philosophical revisions of the postwar years.
In the literary debate, the most heretical thoughts acquired a
distinctly metaphysical, existentialist slant, especially with such
poets as Ole Wivel and Ole Sarvig and in the periodical *Heretica*
of which Bjørnvig was a cofounder. The individualistic, sub-
jective stance found a peculiar expression in Ole Sarvig's sequence
of poems, the central book of which has the title "The I-House."
In the course of the sequence, the individual, anonymous "I"
completes a development reflecting the entire inner history of
modern man as well as the myth of man from innocence, via
the fall and loneliness to a new community through love. The
mystery of natural growth is a basic pattern in the fragmented
metaphoric world of modernity.

If Sarvig strives to gather the severed elements of reality in a
selfmade myth, Erik Knudsen and Ivan Malinovski maintain
the chaotic description, at first in an internationally dominated
imagery, an esthetics of fragmentation. Through an increasingly
energetic disclosure of the social and political reasons for the
unsatisfactory and antihuman conditions of the civilized world,
the two poets gradually became more radical. The almost de-
politicized atmosphere of the Cold War period gave way to
an increasing awareness of the reality of social and political
relations. At first as a general attitude which was termed "cul-

tural radicalism," later in a definite socialist attitude which
became the dominant tendency in the second half of the sixties.
The fragmentation came to be seen as historically determined,
and not as a fundamental condition of existence. For Erik
Knudsen it led to a simplification and a politicizing of the
poetic language, to a dialectics of two kinds of writing, the
one a complex, subjective, the other an engaged satirical poetry.

Around 1960 a new generation of poets and a new protest
against the reification of reality appeared. The strength of this
poetry lay in its very details, in its searching among the *disjecta
membra* of civilization and its mass-produced quotidian life. A
pulsating, recording, confronting poetry, the hallmark of which
is vitality—also in the negative description. A poetry which is
often extremely personal and private in its investigation and
microscopy of physical and biological as well as social and
historical life. It is seldom expressed in large syntheses. Some-
times the analysis strikes upon language which is forced through
atomization into a new expressiveness. In Klaus Rifbjerg clear
examples may be found of the kind of confrontation which has
been mentioned several times. The concept of confrontation was
launched in the title of his collection of poems from 1960. The
poem "Medieval Morning" is an example of the characteristic
regression through the personal and those strata of cultural
history that adhere to us like a feeling of queasiness. A de-
valuation of worthless values to an unconditional attitude whose
meeting with the external world produces new aspects of both
the world and the ego. But the purgative process comes first.
The poem ends with the words: "I forget me."

The meeting with the external world may be extremely simple,
as when Robert Corydon draws a landscape with graphic pre-
cision; or it may be fully orchestrated as when Jørgen Sonne
surgically reveals the development of puberty in "The Fold-out
Men" and shows the unfolding into freedom.

In general, the atomization of language mentioned above
does not lead to simplification, but rather to an open style
where different linguistic spheres cooperate; with Jørgen Gustava

Brandt this is seen in new symbolist fusions. Double exposures and multitracked sequences may make the writing complicated, as in the richly fertile imagination of Uffe Harder. Nausea and idiosyncracies may be used provokingly as means to liberation.

In the course of the decade a characteristic change occurs in the idea of liberation. Gradually, the new poets do away with the belief that poetry is a means to a special kind of cognition. In spite of all experiments, it is possible to remain a prisoner of the intellectual tradition of language. Poetry may then be considered as "texts," as linguistic depictions of the world, valid only as "examples," not as interpretations. Connotations, therefore, are to be precluded, and metaphors and symbols are regarded with suspicion. The poem must emphasize the relation to the reader, it must not be sufficient in itself. For a new experience of community, relations *between* people must be found.

These formal considerations, which are expressed in the texts, gradually became connected with the leftist-socialist political awakening toward the end of the sixties. If the first revolutionary awareness in Danish poetry arrived in a show-boat, the second one was not unrelated to the American warships in the Gulf of Tonkin, and both were expressions of the sickness of the capitalist and industrialized world. On the arena of international politics imperialism became frighteningly visible, there was a growing feeling of language as a means of oppression.

Generally, a change can be felt from a vertical to a horizontal concept of existence. Technically, the interest was moved to words as materials, and for a while a so-called concretist poetry appeared. One of its aims was to demystify the language of poetry. The tendency is suggested in Benny Andersen, whose portraits are made up of puns and tricky ambiguities in such a way that the material aspect of the poem is emphasized. Poetry is language, not illusion. With Vagn Steen the view is programmatic, and in the works of Per Højholt the transition is accomplished from a metaphysical poetry around 1950 to a deliberately aperspectivistic mode of writing. In the theoretical treatise "Cézanne's Method" (1967), a counterpart of Paul la Cour's "Fragments of a Diary," he argued for a poetic practice consisting of the dynamic development of the linguistic material, of its inertia, or, in the words of the painter Cézanne: the idea of art as "an extension of nature into consciousness." Again and again in Højholt's poetry the automatic and random aspects of a verbal sequence are stressed as deliberate disillusionments.

In continuation of the theory and practice of Per Højholt, concretism developed into a conscious philosophy of "writing" which could renounce the illusion completely, either by using popular literature as a pattern (as in Per Kirkeby), by creating a new sensibility of simplification and commonplaces (as in Jørgen Leth), or by means of philosophical sequences far beyond fiction (as in Peter Laugesen). Hans-Jørgen Nielsen began within dogmatic concretism, but in his later works he has attempted to unite the criticism of language with an overtly Marxist criticism of society. The poems of Sten Kaalø and Lean Nielsen testify to new possibilities of formulating direct, personal, and social experience in a more traditional, yet contemporary form. And the sensual subjectivity of Henrik Nordbrandt is strangely related to the experience of a spent world from whose enigmatic remains new modes of existence may be created.

As has already been mentioned, there is a distinct tendency within Modernism toward a depersonalization of the writing subject. As we have shown, however, this does not mean that individualism has given in. Neither did the discovery of the collective unconscious prove a way toward the experience of community. The lyrical poem in which this challenge has been taken up most explicitly, and which has united a new awareness of language with an idea of community, is Inger Christensen's *It* (1969). The poem is about "all those who go on even though it is impossible." The lack of freedom is common to human beings and, therefore, they must seek freedom together. Physical and, hence, psychological reality is shared. She speaks in one place of "our intersubjective conditions, our collective psyche or psychosis, our common prison." The book is a sys-

tematic and symmetrical construction, inspired by e.g. modern
linguistics. The text grows, as it were, out of language in a
creation of "it," an all-encompassing word, a utopia, a dream
of freedom, of being in and among people. The book is not a
statement of ideas, but a function, an attempt at creating a
language which does not *speak* the idea, but which *is* the
relation between human beings.

It is written in an interval between an old and a new world
and speaks, therefore, of the disorder which was established as
a theme at the beginning of the period described here, i.e. in
the views of chaos of Sophus Claussen, Tom Kristensen, and
Otto Gelsted. Inger Christensen says,

> How to integrate the leveled building
> how to put writing into its place in its chaos
> . . . . . .
> How to integrate a world
> which is completely and hopelessly over
>
> in a world that will not begin . . .

That is a contemporary expression of the attempt at keeping
the fragments together. It is no longer a question of the con-
sciousness of the individual, of the interior universe, but a
question of the way from alienation to the freedom of the
community. A community which has not been rendered im-
possible by the tragic conditions of existence, but which has
nearly always been determined or hindered by historically speci-
fied powers.

List of Translators

Robert Fred Bell   R.F.B.
Poul Borum   P.B.
Nadia Christensen   N.C.
Ann Freeman   A.F.
Rolf Gjedsted   R.G.
Kurt Hansen   K.H.
Erik Hansen   E.H.
Uffe Harder   U.H.
R. P. Keigwin   R.P.K.
Carl King   C.K.
Carl Malmberg   C.M.
Lee Marshall   L.M.
Sheila LaFarge   S.L.F.
Else Mathiessen   E.M.
Knud Mogensen   K.M.
Ole Sarvig   O.S.
Ingvar Schousboe   I.S.
Vagn Steen   V.S.
Linda Tagliaferro   L.T.
Alexander Taylor   A.T.
Tania Ørum   T.Ø.
Jørgen Gustava Brandt   J.G.B.
Biographies translated by Tania Ørum
Introduction translated by John Svendsen

NOTE: When no initials are mentioned following a poem, the
   poem was originally written in English.

11

Sophus Claussen
(1865–1931)

S OPHUS CLAUSSEN was a journalist who traveled widely
in Europe and lived for some time in Paris, where he be-
came acquainted with the French symbolists, among others
Stéphane Mallarmé.

He introduced several French authors in Denmark and made
a Danish adaptation of Shelley's *The Sensitive Plant* in 1906.

His chief works of poetry are *Pilefløjter* (Wooden Whistles)
1899, *Djævlerier* (Diableries) 1904, *Danske Vers* (Danish Verse)
1912, *Fabler* (Fables) 1917, and *Heroica* (Heroica) 1925.

In an Orchard

Did storm fall on suncalm surface?
My soul fluttered up like a cloth,
and a lightning-torn cascade of thunder
poured rain over green leaves.
When it grew quiet, you were mine.

Paths are damp among gooseberry-bushes—
and now in the stillness a fragrance rises
from the drenched grass and the countless
cherry blossoms displaying themselves,
pale against an ocean of dazzling air.

Let me wander in here beside you,
dark-eyed delicate virgin;
let your fruit-blossom white
hands slide round my waist;
be my lithe-running vine.

And lean your apple-blossom red
cheek against me, and kiss my mouth.
Your lips are fragrance, sweetness.
But the softest caresses glow
from the dark-shining ground of your eyes.

When I have drawn your arm around my neck
and your breast tight to my heart
so that I hear your gentlest sigh,
then I feel no cold in the dew,
then I grow light, and tremble with joy.

The fruit blossoms lift their splendor
against the sunset blue.
Before me two wondering eyes,
before me your breast and your bare ‐
arm lying around my neck.

The earth is wet to your foot, pure one,
and spiced like the air of the orchard.
Let us kiss in silence and alone!
We ourselves are like two appleboughs:
we shall blossom and bear fruit.

                                                P.B.

Anadyomene

My own soul's goddess, who alone must be obeyed,
whose name is like a balm, fragrant when poured ...

through a spray of memories buried by storm and stream
my Eve Aphrodite has risen from the sea.

On her young face a game of rays is resting.
Like a child she tilts her head to the side and smiles ...

startled, a little dazed by the wind and the wave-beat,
eyes brimming with caresses, good as a spring day.

A braid of ivy winds through her soft, shadowed hair,
while tenderly her brow emerges toward me.

And she is modestly clad in joyful, light garments;
there is a fragrance of violets in her young shadow.

She is as good as the Bible, she is as fine and stern
as an archbishop's sermon printed on vellum.

I fill your air with her light, cool beauty—
the bell in my heart's cathedral ringing for Sunday.

P.B.

Look, I Met in a Street—

Look, I met in a street
Death ... oh, a lovely sight:
brown summer locks,
a damsel's snowy skin.
"Let me live," I begged Death
In my young heart's pain.

"Live for one spring, at peace
beside your virgin snow!
By your chaste side let me live
one spring, though one only,
with kisses that your maiden friend
behind the curtain dare stay to see."

Dressed in sweet lace upon lace
she looked like a meadow in flower.
Behind her shell of beauty
she was winter-hard, dead and stern.
I have asked impossibility
to make my wedding bed.

I have asked impossibility
to put on a wedding gown.

I have begged Death for spring,
therefore I shall be destroyed.

P.B.

Heroica

It is a fight to halt wild horses.
It is a fight to win rare women,
stately, beautiful, who offer fair resistance—
and satisfy them for their loss.

It is a fight to put life-size
figures alive onto canvas,
and a fight to conjure spirit
from compressed worlds into a tight frame.

It is a fight to fell big trees—
but also to make them grow
with wide-spread arms, strong as giants,
and roots deep in the mould—the same whether
raising a tree out of the earth itself
or an artifact of word and color.

It is a fight which delights the whole kingdom
to have checked our own strength
on the point of victory . . .
and a fight to grasp the current of life—
gold coins for one, song for another—
and not lose the right word when its time is there,
while it is still worth knowing.

It is a fight to keep both power and spirit,
and to suffer punishment from no fist.
If condemned, you must stand up to the sentence
with words that have five fingers on each hand.

P.B.

The Flowing out into Infinity

I remember the splash against the bridge piers,
moonlight straight over the waves
and the solitary night over our heads.

I remember that the stream ran past us
while an anchored ship,
stationary, straight out there,
moved its sailless masthead.
I had in me an urge
to flow away on the waves like the moonlight,
or lie down solitary and dark,
to be cradled in the midst of what passes
like the moored ship—a single
steady yet heaving point
at the flowing out into infinity.

Perhaps I dreamed, for a moment without thought,
of being in the dark deserted ship,
of lying in its cold hull, drifting
without sail or oar,
borne by dark waters flowing forever full—

of drifting by the low banks
past inlets and bays
past ferry piers and antique mills,
always in midstream—to end, who knows?
perhaps in some far town with different granaries and wharf rats,
joined somewhere else to the mainland
at the flowing out into infinity.

I had to stay where I was,
but weary of being
a point bobbing ceaselessly before the unlimited,
I began to seek: oh if only
we could draw from the waves' splash under the bridge,
from the measure of the schooner's heavy rigging,
from the dull flickering of moonlight on the waves,
final thoughts, filled
with the motion of the infinite!

P.B.

Johannes V. Jensen
(1873–1950)

JOHANNES V. JENSEN was strongly influenced by his childhood in the countryside in Jutland (Cimberland), by his studies of natural science (Darwin), and by travels in Europe, America and the Far East. For a number of years he contributed essays on travel and popular science to Danish newspapers.

His poetic fame was established by *Digte* (Poems) 1906. Among his other chief works are the historical novel *Kongens Fald* (The Fall of the King) 1900–01, English translation 1933, the evolutionary work *Den Lange Rejse* (The Long Journey) 1908–22, English translation 1922–24, the three volumes of short stories *Himmerlandshistorier* (Himmerland Stories) 1898–1910, and the prose sketches *Myter* (Myths) printed in several volumes between 1907 and 1943.

He was awarded the Nobel Prize in 1944.

At Lunch

Blessed be the café!
Thank God for the velvet corner of the sofa.
I regard my waiter with sympathy,
I sit cool and clean-shaven at the table,
find the rung beneath it with my feet
and stretch my nose toward the tablecloth's chaste smell of
    chlorine.

Give me a beer!
I will sing the praises of the amber beer from the taps.
It's ice-cold and effervescent.
Jesus, how my teeth yearn for it!
My throat begins drinking as soon as I spot it in the distance!

—I want to bury myself in a gulp...
I was thirsty...last night, how did it go?

Now I feel fine.
Four blossoming pieces of smorrebrod in front of me.
          First I eat the one with egg and herring—
Oh, the faint hint of sulphur and of iodine from the ocean's
          seaweed forests!
Then I sink my teeth into one with young and tender roast beef,
and by my growing silent, the taste deepens.
The sausage bouquet of sheep and of oil-dripping machines,
          textile looms, increases my well-being.
The cheese combines the sensation of decay and smoking love
          in my heart.

But now my breast quivers toward the schnapps
which I have poured myself from the ice-cold bottle.
• Look at it sparkle, laughing brightly.
I hold it up like a huge living diamond,
Corn-Akvavit, in short: Denmark!
I sit here preparing myself for the best moment.
It's pleasant here. Hats pass by the window. A lot of people
          are up and about in the street.
I've told myself that life and the solar system are doing very
          nicely.

Skoal!

I do not lodge an angry protest against the earth's waltz between
          the constellations
because I myself am a bench-warmer;
I'd rather light joy out of my heart, gently
along with all the good-time girls and shawms.

Happiness and I didn't understand one another;
I always spoke a dialect wherever I went.
The fact is, I lost Emma.

Why?
Wasn't she gay?
Wasn't she slender, with a graceful curving back,
young and pure appetite like quicklime?
Wasn't her breast full and resilient
like a wicker basket full of fresh-cut clover,
didn't she have slender arms and the brightest teeth,
a maelstrom of dark hair and eyes like gun muzzles?
Why then did I compose a cold lie
about a very important expedition to the Arctic Sea?
Emma, because I do not want to ask a girl
who is no concern of mine except that I happen to love her
to wash her nineteen-year-old body.
I dislike fusel oil, butyric acid and other stinging fluids.
I devour principally girls with nerves in their skin.
You turned up less tidy, although innocent, Emma.
All right, I kept quiet, but I cast you off.
How lucky that about the same time you
displayed an unconquerable distaste for me,
my indomitable head, my delighted egoism, and the entire
            coarseness of my soul!
How healthy for us both that we forthwith hated each other!
Oh, how we frittered each other away. Wildly I traveled to
            the Pole.
You married a violinist
whose fingers did not shun resin
and who later is said to have elicited from you the purest tones.

Well, I lost Emma.
The whole world pitied me. I think I hurt a lot of people
with the cynical lightness with which I consoled myself.
My life is one long compensation.
Who says that one should live happily?
That same spring met me frisky and healthy, ▬
gloomy with longing for love
in the embrace of lovely Olga.

She was always washed and cool.
Maybe she was a maid at a public bath.
(Emma belonged to the more fashionable gentry).
Olga was so free and easy, the clothes whistled off her.
Oh, the soles of her feet were absolutely as fresh and cool
as water-lily leaves in Guldager Brook,
where I swam as a youth.
When Olga came to me she brought in the scent
of wide-open drawers of linen, which I love,
a weather of starch and of purified blued clothes.
Dearest Olga, it was sweet to breathe the cool air around you.
You were as fresh as a sheaf of grain,
and God knows who later garnered you.

I've poured myself a fresh schnapps from the ice-cold bottle.
Without hesitation, I down this one, too.
The schnapps is cold, sweet, strong, and burning...
This was a skoal to the insatiable appetite
that knocks me down and sets me on my feet again
right in the middle of full-hipped strolling miracles in human
        shape.
Are you sorry that I sing so that everything blackens before me?

Ah, Emma and Olga!
Where are you now?
To old good times, then!
I feel a curative warmth, my heart leaps,
I believe I'm happy in spite of the pain.
The schnapps is cold, sweet, strong, and burning...

Skoal!

                                                    A.T.

At Memphis Station

Half-awake and half-dozing,
rammed by a clammy reality but still off
in an inner sea-fog of Danaid dreams,
I stand here my teeth chattering
at Memphis Station, Tennessee.
It's raining.

The night is empty, dull,
and the rain flogs the ground
with a dark witless energy.
Everything is clammy and impenetrable.

Why is the train held up here hour after hour?
Why has my destiny come to a halt here?
Have I fled from the rain and corrosion of soul
in Denmark, Japan, and India
only to be rainbound and rot in Memphis,
Tennessee, U.S.A.?

And now the dawn. Joylessly the light
filters in over the wet prison.
The day ruthlessly exposes
the cold rails and the masses of black mud,
the waiting room with its candy machines,
the orange peels, the stumps of cigars and matches.
The day grins with spewing gutters
and an eternal grille of rain.
Rain, I say, from heaven and to earth.

How deaf and immovable is the world,
how talentless the creator!

And why do I keep on paying my dues
to this plebian Kneipp-cure of an existence!

Quiet! Look how the engine,
that mighty machine, stands there calmly seething,
wrapping itself in smoke—it is patient.
Light your pipe on an empty stomach.
Curse God and swallow your pain!

All right then, stay in Memphis!
Your life's not anything but a sour rain
anyway, and it was always your destiny
to hang around delayed in some
miserable waiting room or other—
Stay in Memphis, Tennessee!

For in one of those poster-howling buildings
happiness waits for you, happiness,
if you can only swallow your impatience.
Here, too, sleeps a shapely young virgin,
her ear buried in her hair.
She will come to meet you
on the street one fine day
like a wave of fragrance
with an air as if she knew you.

Isn't it spring?
Doesn't the rain fall lushly?
Doesn't it sound like an amorous murmur,
➤ a long, hushed love-chat,
➤ mouth against mouth
between the rain and the earth?
The day dawned so sorrowfully,
but look how the rainfall brightens!

Will you not give day its right to battle?
Anyway, it's light now. The smell of mould

sets in among the rusted iron braces of the platform
mixed with the rank breath of the rain-dust—
a premonition of spring—
consoling, isn't it?

And now look, look how the Mississippi
in its bed of flooded forests
wakes to the day!
Look how the huge river revels in its turnings!
How royally it gushes in its bending and swings rafts
of trees and battered driftwood in its eddies.
Look how it sweeps a gigantic paddle-wheeler
in its deluge embrace
like a dancer who is lord of the floor! ✭
Look at the sunken headlands—oh, what overwhelming
                    primeval peace
over the landscape of drowning forests!
Can't you see how the current's morning water
dresses itself for miles in day's simple light
and wanders hale and hearty under the pregnant clouds!

Now, compose yourself, you implacable man!
Will you never forget that you were promised eternity?
Will you begrudge the earth your meager gratitude?
And then what will you do with your lover's heart? ✭

Pull yourself together, and stay in Memphis,
show up in the square as a citizen,
go in and insure yourself with all the others,
pay your premium of sleaziness
so they needn't fear anything from you,
and you won't get tossed out of the club.
Go court that virgin with roses and ring of gold
and start a sawmill like other men.
Hitch up your rubber boots in peace . . .
Gaze out, puffing your wise pipe
in sphinx-forsaken Memphis . . .

Ah, here comes the wretched freight train
for which we have waited six hours.
It comes in slowly—with shattered sides,
it whistles weakly, the cars staggering on three wheels
and the shattered box-cabins dripping earth and mud.
But on the tender among the coal
four still forms are lying
covered by bloodwet coats.

Then our huge engine snorts,
edges forward a little and stops, deeply sighing,
and stands crouched for the leap. The track is clear.

And we travel on
through the flooded forests
under the gaping sluices of the rain.

                                        A.T.

Otto Gelsted
(1888–1968)

OTTO GELSTED did journalistic work for the Communist press and studied the Greek and Roman Classics. He translated, among others, Aristophanes, Euripides, Homer, and Sigmund Freud.

Among his chief works are the collections of poems *Jomfru Gloriant* (Miss Gloriant) 1923, *Rejsen til Astrid* (The Journey to Astrid) 1927, *Henimod Klarhed* (Towards Clarity) 1931, and *Emigrantdigte* (Emigrant Poems) 1945.

Carriage Ride

I feel it still, like a patch of sun:
the gentle pressure of your knee. ▪
Sitting close in a one-horse carriage,
we traveled homeward leisurely.

The Pleiades' misty swarm of stars,
the light touch of your soft knee!
Round us, the land, the fields and houses
stretched as far as we could see.

But there among our Jutland fields
on that jolting carriage ride,
I was lifted into a heavenly parish
by a knee's warm pressure by my side. ▪
N.C.

The Show Boat

The ship heads straight into harbor
at shadowy dusk.
Her megaphone bellows salute to the city,
the electric searchlights
level their five-splintered beams
up in the air like a comet's tail
and scrawl in firescript on the clouds:
      BUY A FORD

And the ship is transformed
to a garish glitter of lights from end to end;
airmen bombard her with bengal-lights;
the funnel shaped like a bottle of Tuborg,
and the daubed sides with their colossal figures and lettering
            like a fantastic camouflage,
the Kodak girl, Johnnie Walker, and the rest of them,
alternate in dazzling colors
that are mirrored in the water...
till the ship is riding, now in a green abyss,
now in a blaze of yellow flickering flame,
now in a pool of blood.

And on board—what is there not on board?
Here are exhibits of painting and cooking,
French cuisine and cubism and chemical recipes;
here is the Social Exhibition showing society in longitude,
from the proletarian eaten up by lice in a dustbin
to the *toilette de luxe* of the millionaire.

Here are clinics for make-up and bureaus for suicide,
which men in despair can consult for a suitable fee;

here are displayed the latest stunts of the doctor's art,
men changed into women and women into men;
here is the ship herself with all that's in vogue:
tennis courts and swimming pools, the church and the newspaper
        office
(that prints you the whole Bible in installments);
here is the giant gyroscope,
whose 180,000 revolutions to the minute
neutralize all motion
and safeguard the passengers from seasickness.

And here finally are the passengers—
all of them symbols of sensation and publicity.
The 136-year-old patriarch from Volhynia,
who was with Napoleon at Moscow,
the 6-year-old chess genius, Sammi Meyer, from Poland,
and the Siamese Twins. . . .
Then, of course, an adequate selection
of the world war's bankrupt monarchs and celebrities,
plus—among the crew and the galley staff—
the inevitable Russian grand dukes
and opera queens from Vienna.

And, in the first class,
film stars:
the Hero from the Wild West
(with Odol smile),
the World Comedian
(with Odol smile)
and the Sunbathing Beauty
(Odol smile).

But away up the harbor
sits a man in a shanty
in front of a table with contraptions and clock dials.
He has a shag-pipe in his mouth

and looks like an ordinary blond Danish student.
He is waiting for the moment
when the ship comes over the right spot.
Then he will press a button.

It is not fire from heaven he is waiting for;
no, he himself will raise fire from the abyss.
And in the midst of the popular shimmy,
"Shake me till I shiver,"
while a man of fire strides forth on the show boat
and proclaims a new truth to all mankind—
      OMA IS BEST—
a crash is heard . . .

R.P.K.

Tom Kristensen
(1893–1974)

TOM KRISTENSEN was one of the most distinguished literary critics of the century in Scandinavia; he also introduced and translated world literature of the interwar period, such as D. H. Lawrence, Ernest Hemingway, Ezra Pound, T. S. Eliot, André Gide, and James Joyce.

His most important work as a poet are several volumes of poems written between 1920 and the middle of the thirties and ranging stylistically from cubism to expressionism and a modern classicism: *Fribytterdrømme* (Freebooter Dreams) 1920, *Verdslige Sange* (Worldly Songs) 1927, *Mod den yderste Rand* (Towards the Farthest Edge) 1936.

His great novel *Hærværk* (*Havoc*) 1930, has been translated into several languages including English (1966).

The Execution

Look, for the third time the headsman
wipes the blood and wet from his sword,
and three flames stand up
on the cloth he's used;
but I've no head and I'm dead
when for the sixth time the flame
lights up, lights up
on the headsman's cloth.

We kneel down, we twenty men,
with our heads stretched out,
and I'll see the glittering sword
strike the heads from five;

31

but the sixth time, the sixth time,
when time grows deathly long,
the eye closes,
it's all gone.

Now for the fourth time the headsman
polishes his sword with that cloth,
while number four tumbles down
and the blood jumps out,
and the headsman takes a step closer:
I can make out a dragon coiled
on the hilt-guard
of his sword.

Then I turn my head a little
and see him look up, gray—
shaven hair, bare pigtail—
against the blue sky.
I note each hair that grows
in the headsman's nose and eyebrows.
Now I see, and I see
more and more.

Now for the fifth time the headsman
wipes the blood and wet from his sword,
and the head of number five
has stopped at his foot;
but time stretches endlessly
before the sixth time, the sixth time.
I no longer believe anything
is going to happen.

Has the world stopped altogether?
Is the sword wet clear through?
Will the headsman wipe it forever
and never put it to use?

My neck keeps hurting, and pain
strikes a running wreath
around the flesh of my throat.
Could I be dead?

No, the headsman is still sighting
down the fine hard edge of the sword.
Then he takes his next step, and stops,
measures, moves back a little.
I see a beetle safely wandering:
metallic green on vaulted back,
it's walking toward
a headsman's foot.

– – –

P.B.

Grass

The grass is strangely tall to me,
lying with my nose to the earth.
If I bow down as low as I can
my world grows high.

Under the pointed greenish gates
I stop. Here I shall stay.
I dare not lose my way
in the shining dark!
I dare not lose
my way among straw!

Inside the dawning halls of the straws
there is a voice waking, calling
in rising notes: comest thou now,
comest thou, comest thou, comest thou now,
thou now.

And as answer
sounds a bright
full of delight boyish bright voice in me:
No, oh not yet! No, oh not yet!
But when my madness is gone,
when my dreams of greatness are gone,
then I shall come, then I shall come,
then I'll be small and happy enough.

P.B.

Fear

Fear is strong as a Mongol horde.
It is ripened by immature years.
And each day my heart grows heavy,
Foreseeing the continents flooded with tears.

But my fear must be vented in longing,
In visions of horror and stress.
I have longed for the final disaster,
For havoc and violent death.

I have longed to see cities burning
And the races of mankind in flight—
A world rushing headlong in panic
From God's retribution and might.

C.M.

It's Knud Who Is Dead
(Knud Rasmussen, the Greenland Explorer)

Today if I were a grouse I'd lift my wing to beat,
and I'd fill my lungs with air and fly through night and day
over a wintry ocean blackening beyond whitish foam,
through the deep December's cloud-tossed space.

Nothing but a grouse in the storm, the toy of all winds,
but I'd fly with a message of tempest into the Northwest.
Heart bursting with pain, I would conjure from my breast
the song that soon will howl like a storm along Greenland's coast.

And farther on it would resound over half of the earth,
follow the footsteps of kamiks and long trails of sledges,
howl across Hudson Bay, on out to King William's Land,
whisper in every settlement along the edge of the earth.

All his old friends would be shaken out of their sleep then,
Willow-Twig and Clearing, Auá with the snow-white dog,
all the lovely girls with wide and shining smiles
would leap up startled, forgetting their untroubled rest.

They should all be wakened. Sorrow has hardly begun.
Soon it will spread to the farthest point of Alaska.
The great Enchanter is dead! The great Magician is dead!
Do you all hear my song? Did you understand what it said?

Islands and countries and rivers lie locked in chains of ice.
The joy that warmed all of you, the burning joy is put out.
Freeze, as the rest of us are freezing today without fire or spark,
for now he's dead. It's Knud who is dead.
Do you understand?

P.B.

William Heinesen
(1900)

WILLIAM HEINESEN was born in Torshavn on the Faroe islands, but although his daily language is Faroese he writes in Danish. He is a painter, musician, and poet.

He started as a poet in the twenties and has with long intervals published poems as well as short stories and novels.

Among his most important novels are *De Fortabte Spillemænd* (*The Lost Musicians*) 1950 (American edition, Twayne, 1971), and *Moder Syvstjerne* (*The Kingdom of the Earth*) 1952 (American edition, Twayne, 1974). Represented in the collection of short stories *Faroese Short Stories*, tr. and ed. Hedin Brønner (Twayne, 1972), he is dealt with at length in *Three Faroese Novelists* by Hedin Brønner (Twayne, 1973).

Hymnus Amoris
Anna Magdalena and Johann Sebastian Bach piae memoriae

FANTASIA
"In thousands of years,
yes, in millions of years
I shall say to you:
Do you know where you are?
You are in my heart."

FUGA
"Yes!" I will answer with joy
from the timeless heavenly realms where I wander:
"I am in your heart,
and I am so happy!

"I am the salt in your blood,
the ancient taste of the sea whence you came,

"I am the everlasting tide
of night and day in your eyes
which the light created
and they recreated the light
and gave it content.

"I am the labyrinth in your ear,
the anvil and the hammer
that gently beats the world's raw material of sound
and grants it meaning.

"I am the airy breeze
that goes through the crowns of your lungs,
the oxygen and the carbon dioxide
as they eternally interchange
with the homely verdure of the earth.

"I am the moisture in your mouth,
the taste buds on your tongue,
the acid in your stomach's flask,
the power in your viscera
that extract the essence of the earth's kernel
and satisfy the myriads of living cells
in your body.

"I am the deep mystery of creation
in your inner sanctum
in whose darkness the moon
rises and sets unseen.
I am the lonely young fruit
on your womb's ancient Yggdrasil
and I am the spring of the milk
in your breasts.

"I am the substance in your bones,
the litheness in your sinews and joints,
the horn in your hair and your nails.
And I am the fiery fragrance
from the pores of your skin.

"I am the vehemence
in your arteries' mountain streams
and the meekness
in the blue delta of your veins.
I am the white hot energy
in the lightning branches of your nerves,
yes, I am life's electric potential
in your soul.

"I am the fearless teeth in your smile
when you are glad.
I am the tender secret sweetness in your sorrow.
I am the whirling fire in your fear,
and the fury of my love
shall burn your grief to ashes!"

I.S.

Rain in Leningrad

It is raining in the bright gray evening
on mirror-wet streets,
on the bay and the misted river.
The grass quivers quietly on the graves of the dead
under the everlasting rain.

Everywhere in the pouring damp
there are young trees in full leaf
planted by the people of the city
after the end of the war and the victory
and the bitter losses.
Each man and each woman and each child
his green tree of hope.

In the Winter Palace there is a hall
of pure gold.
Today it was filled with silent staring people.
Tonight the gold is alone
behind rain-wet windowpanes in the dark hall.

                                                    A.T.

The Ascension of J. H. O. Djurhuus, Poet

Gray evening.
Chugging engines. Unloading of fish.
Kids on their cold way back from games on the beach
to fireplace and supper.
The tills are checked in little shops.
The jugs are filled in the chapels
for that evening's preachers.
The forecast says gales.
Life rolls on
and all is normal,
except that a strange old man has been seen
in a flapping gown with a harp on his shoulder.
Somebody a bit peculiar?

It was J. H. O. Djurhuus, the bard.
He got out of bed this night
and picked up his harp
and went west.
He left his dead body in the bed.

He was a strange man, was Djurhuus.
The things he would do!
A bit of a bother at times,
he didn't fit in all too well.
He was up in his Latin and Greek
and knew his literature, even the foreign.
A practicing lawyer, what's more
but sometimes too big for his boots
—and a bit too fond of his booze.
He had words to size up the worthies
a bull's-eye each time.

And his laughter, his roars of laughter,
could be quite frightening
not to say downright rude.
But now he's gone—ah well, ah well
We all come to that.

An old wise woman saw him go,
taking off like a big black bird
going west,
disappearing in the dusk.
Needless to say only few believed it.

Still that doesn't make it any less true.
What that aged crone had seen
WAS the soul of our bard and translator of Homer
on the mighty wings of gale and darkness—
—delivered from the spite and the worldly vulgarity
of petty small-town narrowness—
—on mighty wings borne hence.

Gone over rock and sea
gone west gone west
gone to Hesperian faraway shores
where day never ends
and myths can live immortal lives
far above and away from the trivial round.

The forecast gale
cut loose at ten.
Then it was sea and sea again.
‑The oceanids' millions cavorted in the froth of the waves.
The bard struck his huge harp
(with hidden echoes of ballads and Ossian's poems,
but also of Pindar and Ovid)
and he sang to the gusts.
His strong dark song

resounded for miles on the Northern waves
and may in time, when the time is ripe
fill all his Northern world.

Poseidon lifted his surly head.
Medusa, released from her petrified curse,
for a moment hid her face in her hands.
The ghostly singer was met by the Hesperides
and taken along to their glorious grove,
where Ladon, the dragon, guards the apples of gold
that confer eternal youth.

K.H.

Paul La Cour
(1902–1956)

PAUL LA COUR was a poet and art critic. He wrote chiefly about Danish and French artists and poets; he translated among others Camus, Garcia Lorca, Anouilh, Girandoux, René Char, and edited Cézanne's and Gauguin's letters and selections of Baudelaire's criticism.

By introducing poets such as Paul Eluard and by his personal poetics *Fragmenter af en Dagbog* (Fragments of a Diary) 1948, he has had great influence on poets, critics, and painters of the "forties."

He published several volumes of poetry in the twenties and later, but his breakthrough came with the last three books, *Levende vande* (Living Waters) 1946, *Mellem bark og ved* (Between Bark and Wood) 1950, and *Efterladte digte* (Posthumous Poems) 1957.

The Unforeseen

Wet flows the air
through the dark sailing swarm of leaves.
Something that was taken from me,
something filling my soul,
streams back in here again.
Only what breaks the bounds,
the dream that heeds nothing,
the light that imagination
wound around the world,
will feed without end your mind.
Only in the unforeseen
the soul was not blind.

P.B.

She Could not Fall

In swallow wing
I waited,
on tree bough where
her feet lingered,
in light warmth of grass,
by the willows, on the water,
on the bright stones.
Down narrow paths she came,
young girl, stranger.
the shadow on her mouth,
the silence on her shoulder,
stronger than beauty,
younger than courage.
She came stepping on the deep;
the wave she set foot on
became a wide road;
she carried me, though I
was the path she took.
My life was changed:
she could not fall.

                                      P.B.

The Tree

The squirrel, the birds left my crown
when the rock I stood on fell;
now the harpstrings of my roots hang
toneless in the air, one last rift
in the rock wall clutching a root.
The beetles still creep on my trunk—
a final tiny flame of life—
and I have hidden behind my own leaves,
holding them out toward the last storm,
itself hidden behind light of distant horizons,
humble and still, scarcely existing.
O you who bind the living and the dead
to this great strange game
your will be done.
Let the air heal its path behind me,
but before I fall let me sing,
let me once in eternal song
be faithful: close to your lives
live bound one last time. Wholly free . . .

                                        P.B.

Threshold

My four elements: the birds, the trees, the grass, and the sea.
What swings in lightness, the always faithful green rock of
purity, the eternity of return, and what rests in flowing change.
I have laid their clover against our wounds. You might heal
if you wanted to. Your melancholy is a miser: it dare not live
itself out to the full. If you throw yourself into the fire, where
God's mangrip burned down, then I am not your singer. I dare
to smile, dare to wait, dare to sing out what is hidden from
me. Lay your hands together. We shall be found when the seas
are healed. Future is playing on our threshold.

                                        P.B.

Peloponnesian Nights

I

Here I followed the path in,
heard the grasshoppers scraping,
the light feet of the river
walking the chalk-gray stones.
The light failed over the
stagecoaches of snails,
the fires of bees, the warm
broad mountains'
worn-down hives.
I saw the evening falcon
in the resin-dark air,
above the mulberries of the threshing-floor,
a hunger-sword of cold.
Fell me whenever you please ⸱
while I am still thirst,
while I love and am thirst,
while a hand is a leaf
and a leaf is still happiness,
seize me like a bird of the woods,
embrace me not cold. Not death's quick
boy's arms are evil;
bitter only the void's
limp tongue of sand.

II

The birds fall silent, and the leaves,
whose thorny tongues never
sang. The beetles, the bees,
the mole in its galleries
are asleep. No breeze
plays with bright fingers
on the harpstrings of reeds,
no vein of night opens,

trickling, no piping
sounds of free-leaping
waters. Long ago the river
forsook its stones.
Falcons are flying around
the fragrant breast of the mountain
in the evening. Lonely, a stranger. Alone.
Life will soon be over.
What, oh what do you
want from me then here
⁓ in the land of perfection,
seacold impatient shining young cry of
spring, of holy spring
in my honed
winter boughs?

P.B.

Faint Horn-sound of Summer

Faint horn-sound of summer
lightly fading beyond the wood—
the hushed calm of ripeness
looms up before my eye.
Then plow me, plow me, drive me
through my last metamorphosis,
bestow on me with rain-cold
hands the last chill courage.
Take my features. Worn out long ago.
Belonged to someone else. No one
will breathe behind them and wait.
Fill me with winter, with sun and snow,
O hale mountains which I have yet to see:
I shall not return.

P.B.

Nis Petersen
(1897–1943)

NIS PETERSEN was influenced by a pietist environment; he was a journalist and a tramp. Inspired by Irish and Nordic folk poetry, he had a strong influence on the young generation in the thirties.

His great historical novel *Sandalmagernes Gade* (*The Street of the Sandal Makers*) 1931 (English edition, 1932), and his novel about the Irish War of Independence *Spildt Mælk* (Spilt Milk) 1934, are his best known prose works.

Among his collections of poems are *Nattens Pibere* (Pipers of the Night) 1926, and *En Drift Vers* (A Drove of Verse) 1933.

Spring at Mariager Fjord

Two golden butterflies found one another,
And eight golden wings bore them away;
One tiny wood mouse found another,
And they—well, they were tempted by Satan,
And life is so—all too all too short.

Madonna basted with silken threads
So deftly that strands were flying all around.
Two woodpeckers mated so woodpecker-bold
That the cuckoo began virtuously to prophesy
A nest full of woodpecker-bold things.

Primroses and anemones sprang up,
And orchids sprang from the loins of the earth.
There came hundreds of millions

49

Of gay, merry flower-women
And gay, merry flower-men.

For it was spring and there was noise-making
In every glade made light by the sun
And on a grass pillow amidst the warmth
Sat the blacksmith's daughter with unbuttoned blouse
And sewed away on a little dress.

L.M.

Two Little Old Widows Playing Duet

Twenty fingers—twenty busy bees
—white fingers over gray keys
—twenty busy white bees fetching
honey tunes.

Two little childish brittle voices
buzzing after the white bees
—diving—fetching sweet tunes
from hidden places.

Notes—drop after drop splashing
—toppling chains of tinkling notes
—two little old ladies on a music stool.

Just a moth-eaten elderly spinet
—just two twittering little white widows
through the smoke of my cigaret.

P.B.

Elegy 1940

They asked me: live your life as before
when springtime was a feast and a glow.
For now the sap is in stalk and in bud
and fruit in the bosoms of the flowers.
But ah, somewhere in Flanders
a brain is made into mush.

They asked me in for joy and feast,
to flute and trumpet sound.
A full and noble wine they poured
in a crystal glass for me.
But ah, at Narvik at this moment
a young man died.

They asked me to forget it all,
the gloom, the evil, and the need—
for who can reach what steel and fire
committed against these youths.
But ah, I see a battlefield
of flayed human flesh.

P.B.

Jens August Schade
(1903)

JENS AUGUST SCHADE has lived the life of an authentic
bohème—at times without even having a roof over his head.
He had his first poem published in 1925 and since then
he has published a large number of poems. These as well as
his novels and plays are all inspired by a pan-erotic attitude
with quite surprising surrealistic aspects and an expressionism
which shocked the bourgeoisie in the interwar period.

His novel *Mennesker Mødes og Sød Musik Opstår i Hjertet*
(People Meet And Sweet Music Fills the Heart) 1944, has been
filmed and shown in many countries.

Several of his poems have been translated into English and
French.

The Heavenly Sun

As the heavenly sun
arranged the clouds in angles and circles
in the evening back home in Jutland
my verses
take form

they say of me
that I was born in a place
called Skive—I do not remember
I am looking toward another sky

I have forgotten my age
for stars and storms in the night

P.B.

52

Changed Eyes

The streets don't have much to say

I was walking down a street of a fatal suburb
among women with twilight eyes

I was looking for a girl

now I go around so lonely
let me tell you the song
you are far away but I remember

give me a new world
peaceful conditions—we all feel it
how bad we need something to believe in

It's full of living hands
they have told me
that all is well

we remember by night some old friends
one is in Paris—where are all the others
we'll meet I'm sure in a song-filled night
with changed eyes

P.B.

Woman

Of gold and fire is the feast of my thought—
why then is fear in your heart?
behind your breasts flowers are growing
you smell of apples and eternity

P.B.

Equinox

But our glance was turned inward
while we slept

it is us now
before death unfolds
great flower of the heart—
you're trembling
yes we love—
~ young people wear no clothes

P.B.

My Young Love

My young love left me alone we do not remember
how
like a ship fading out in a blue horizon
like a dying note she disappeared
and sleep came to me and the earth grew distant
like a singing globe of silver

but you have appeared to me in my dreams
your voice was a cooling rain
your mouth a fruit ripe for eating
made for a hungry man
I remember you sadly and it soothes me
like a song of birds and trees

they exist those women who love a man
like a meal they love to eat . . .

P.B.

The Wonderful Vase

The wonderful vase—with an eternal grasshopper
every day standing still in the same place
among dark green straws. Behind it the moon
and a little dark temple. There I'd like to sit,
if only I could sleep and lie down in the picture—
and watch the shining moonbeams on every little house
in the dark neighborhood. And listen to the sounds
of the trembling grasshopper's immortal playing.

P.B.

Nocturnal Ride

Now the moon turns up behind green trees—
now the moon turns down behind green trees—
now a girl comes into the searchlight—
she is dressed.—I still feel the thrill

flashing through me when her knee hit
my eye. And her black dress fluttered.
A billygoat was standing trustfully at the wayside
looking at stars. It has seen plenty

in *its* little life. The bleating and calling
of the goat still sound in my ear.
A crucifix at the roadside was standing on its head
when I turned round and watched it under my arm,

and the girl's dress was still fluttering. Big and red the moon
hung between her legs.—A little church
disappeared between them. And the searchlights
of the car are shining now in the firmament.

P.B.

Snow

Well, then, the snow finally came,
and I almost thought it'd never start snowing,
and now it honestly seems we'll have a real pile of snow,
and not keep going around thinking of snow forever without
    it coming

The *air* has snow in it, too,
it's sort of *loaded* with snow,
there could be a heavy snowfall far away,
which you kind of *felt* inside,
without actually *knowing* it,
but it's *coming*, so that you can see it.

All the time I was hoping for snow,
oh, it's fun that it came.
Yes, now it's lying there—
look, how white it is,
hot damn! it makes me feel good,
all the time I really believed it would come.

And now all at once it's lying there—
isn't it funny that it comes like that
without your doing anything about it,
I didn't pull it out of the air,
it just sort of came by itself.

P.B.

I Love You

Around me lies
the sky from all sides,
I love you, light space,
long night of stars,
splashing fire from inside yourself, •
and planets ripening like apples on a mystic tree.

P.B.

The Bureau

These lacquer birds singing in the bureau—
these secretive Chinese sunshine gods
who painted in them a picture of themselves—
it is as though millennia were singing in my body
it's so much alive!
I sit here and look at the bureau,
and suddenly it starts singing
and opening up,
and I feel all the gods of China,
in a chorus around me
open up
and sing with young calm.

P.B.

At the Movies

We two criminals who love to go to the movies
while thousands are working with gas and jam
and weird things like income tax forms,
we feel simultaneously like gangsters and kings,
• breaking, in that way, the rules of the world
and sitting and breathing into each others' ears
doing silly things
at the movies,
looking at the pictures
and touching your legs under your dress,
laying your hand on my arm and gazing romantically up
                        into the heaven of the hall,
while pictures are trailing past—and becoming strange,
loosening the bodies, and doing other things
while the world trails past up there on the stage,
closing our eyes and thinking of other things, while they kiss
a subdued movie kiss up there, the innocence
of which touches us deeply, its purity of mind,
because it is acting. It is absolutely not real,
they are paid for it, they make money that way,
while we're sitting and doodling and doing it for real,
in this way we are criminals in a busy world, catching
the great inspiration from mechanical kisses
• for a real show back home in our own little high-barbaric theater.
                                                    P.B.

A *Strawberry*

The secret mysterious feeling
of touching a strawberry in my mouth
can never be bought with money.

One doesn't know the reason,
but a strawberry can make one's soul
glow all the way down to the bottom.

I am so happy for this
strawberry I got this morning
that I heard space saying

the loveliest things I have tasted.

P.B.

Hulda Lütken
(1896–1946)

HULDA LÜTKEN published a number of collections of poems from 1927 to 1945 illustrating the tension between desire and purity. Her ecstatic art with its romantic feeling for nature is influenced by German expressionism.

Among her best-known collections are *Lys og skygge* (Light and Shadow) 1927, *Klode i drift* (Planet Adrift) 1941, and *Skærsilden* (Purgatory) 1945.

The Moon Mother

One night as a child I saw a strange sight:
I woke.
There was light in the living room.
The moon was shining...

Suddenly I saw my mother:
She stood in the middle of the room,
her face turned toward the window.
She had on the old, gray housedress
that she wore when I was a child.

Her presence was overwhelming;
her head reached up toward the ceiling.
She stood motionless
like a statue of maternity—
like the picture
of eternal motherhood.

Then suddenly I saw her
raise her arms above her head—

as though invoking an unseen power.
And then the moon poured
a stream of light through the window.
It struck her
like a torrent of silver.

She stood motionless
for a moment
in the moonbath,
her arms raised high above her head—
invoking the unseen powers,
glistening,
unforgettable—
like a silver statue—
a shining moon mother.

Then she was gone—
the room was empty.
I ran to my mother's bed:
In the moonlight, I could just see her:
She was fast asleep.
Her breast rose and fell
in peaceful sleep:
not the slightest unevenness of breath to show
that her soul had been out that night
on one of its endless expeditions—
invoking the eternal God.

God made our soul secret—
that our body might breathe in peace.

N.C.

Johannes Wulff
(1902)

JOHANNES WULFF was born in Copenhagen. He studied German and French at the University. He is an imaginative essayist, poet and novelist, his social engagement being influenced by a Christian outlook.

He has been especially praised for his novels *Oh, Ungdom* (Oh, Youth) 1929 and *Katten der fik feber* (The Cat that Caught a Fever) 1952 and for his poetry, published in several volumes from the late twenties to the seventies.

The Friend Is Dead

Man, are you
all alone, man
that's what you said
then when you talked
then when alive
then when
so many were alive—

since then, that's true,
more than many died
since then we huddle up
in the wind
and hold our hands
before our faces in the rain
and we cower in front
of evening fires
with hollow coughs
until midnight lightning

with tiger eyes
outside the window pane
and singing of rats
under scullery floors—
— — —
Far too few violets
are given away
violets for young
ladies in the town
with whom you discovered
angels in the cloud
and spring so early
in February—

The poor man you shared
your meal with
I have lots of greetings
from him as well
he still hides and steals
along the walls
on his journey from right
to left—and back.—

The young ladies
the poor men
they keep asking me
when you're coming again!

He comes every time
there's spring in the cloud
and men dance about
with angels in town
till at last we see
that angels are girls
so man
is not alone—

— —

It is not lonely
under your tree
near the grave

the pipe you once gave me
I'm puffing on now
under the little tree
near the grave.

Then you say:
well, it's like this you see
I got my pay in the morning sun—

I'm now in a place
where clothes are pressed
and shirts are washed
—at Snowwhite's place

and then I take a steam
and sweat bath
and they perfume
my neck and face

and then I buy clothes
at Bargain Fair
and they've got to be blue
like the sky today

we'll meet at Cafe Eternity
where I secretly love
the landlord's daughter
it's a secret to her as well

— — —

I'm very busy
so don't be late

so don't be lost
in thought there

I'm ever so
frightfully busy today

and I also must pay
old debts

so go to Cafe
Eternity
and wait for me there
till I come—

                                        K.H.

Ecstasy of the Flesh

A woman's face was rapt
in the ecstasy of the flesh •
now she was happy enough
to shriek.

She thought:
no, not on my life
that's enough from you
are you out of your mind
you my man
you my unneeded friend.

I'll scream I'll shriek.
I'll spirit myself out
into the world.
I'll be a tree
and I'll be in bloom,
I'll be a baby
and I'll cry.

I cry, I laugh,
I shriek—
my womb's a volcano
for the brave one
who bores right through
to the equator

I'll repent and die
like a doll

with a cloth before my mouth
and a star in my brow.

Oh, you bull from a mountain
as high as your revenge,
you manly man

with a thrusting rod
of the force
of each and every morning

of each sun which rises
with blasts in the trumpet of light
with a hardness divine
right out to my
most faraway toe
and into one well-burnished end
—
I'll perish with pleasure
so overjoyed
and far from death.

Oh. I deserved no
better
than simply the worst
you knew

you my man of a man
who stuns me skillfully
and blissfully
in my snowwhite limbs

so I have no idea
that I live
or didn't know
until now
when it's late too lovely late
to repent
—
It is now too late
to be oneself

Yes, more than that hopping
tail in the air
can be a chicken
under the wheel
of the butcherman's
van.
—
Are you hopping all right
you hopping master
and knight
—

Wish I were humble enough
for your mastering pride
you shamelessly glorious rider •
—
Oh, I'm reaping
my defeat right in
with one knee and the other
while you're trumpeting me
free from above

with hippo snorts
from your open nose
like a preaching priest
who will not be stopped.

— — —

Well, well I must say
I've been properly led to the altar
and all the way through
clerically clean
like for Easter.

A bleating lamb
was led to the slaughter
and you cut me up limb after limb
with an unruly grin
between your tangled hair
and your Assyrian stump of a beard

—

Still threshing along
you insatiable
on your inveterate wench
here in the oldest
of old and natural dark
while the sun is black
and only the moon is white
like I am

Oh, how I sense
that I'm always alive
and never can die.

My knight
my impetuous rider
my hopping hopla-hero.

— — —

Now don't be sad
now that it's over
smile, man, smile
you came out the winner

and my needed friend—

if you turn your eyes from me now
I'll be tired to death with sadness
and shame and anger.

K.H.

Gustaf Munch-Petersen
(1912–1938)

G USTAF MUNCH-PETERSEN was a poet and surrealist painter. He wrote poems in Danish, Swedish, and English, served as a volunteer in the International Brigade during the Spanish Civil War, and was killed at the battle of Ebro.

His chief volumes of poems were *Det Nøgne Menneske* (Naked Man) 1932, *det underste land* (The Land Below) 1933, and *19 digte* (Nineteen Poems) 1937.

The Land Below
for fannie hurst

o great bliss
great bliss have those
who are born in the land below—
everywhere you can see them
walking
loving
crying—
everywhere they go,
but in their hands they carry small objects
from the land below—
— — —
o greater than all countries
more glorious
is the one below—
earth writhes upward
to a peak—
and downward

outward the heavy
living blood sinks
into the land below—

— — —

slender cautious feet
and thin limbs
and the air is pure
over the open climbing roads—
in closed veins
longing is burning in those
who were born up there under the sky—

but o
you should go to the land below—!
o you should see the people of the land below,
where the blood runs freely among them all—
men—
women—
children—
where joy and desolation and love
heavy and ripe
shine in all colors toward the earth—
o the earth keeps secrets like a forehead
in the land below—

— — —

everywhere you can see them
walking
loving
crying—
their faces are locked,
on the inside of their souls there is soil
from the land below—

                                                    P.B.

At the Bottom

nobody knows what he wants –
the good are timid –,
the strong are devils –,
the wise are barren –,
the fertile seduced
to geld their fruits –
– where are you,
where are you tenderness, certainty –?
where
are you hiding –,
where do you hide –,
in readiness for
us who don't know what we seek –?

The Special Miracle

every night he was tired,
and every day he did as he was told –
and without alarm
he grew thirty years old –
and rather alone –

then one night he was not sleepy,
and that night he thought,
that something
might happen to him –
especially –

and early in the morning
he stole five pounds,
and got together with a woman, he knew,
rather drunk –
the day, the night and the next day –

and late in the evening
he got caught –
quietly, without alarm –
and after a time came back –
but oh –!

every night he slept,
and by day he did as he was told –
and together with the woman, he knew,
he quietly grew sixty
years old –
when speaking of life,
he smiled –

Portrait

when sleeping
I seek my princess –,

in the morning
I break all the flowers –,

in the sun
I build my aloneness –,

towards night
I carve out the future –,

my life I spare –
my death
shall never exist –

A Little Song

I have killed mary ann's god –
mary ann dreads my god –
I love mary ann –
when the burning blackness stands out before me
I leave mary ann
to her love of me –

when the pale sun rises
with its blue morning-wet eyes,
I return to mary ann
with my love of her –
poor mary ann –
and poor me –
but we have a great heart
together –
mary ann and I –

Song of the Council

the name of our
wisdom is wine and dance
and silence –
the name of the great hunger
is the same –
the goddess of wisdom
is always alone,
and always drunk
and always she feels
the far-off rhythm of the unknown
teasing her pride, binding
her tongue, releasing
the voices of her listening blood –
we'll protect her aloneness
and shield her silence,
her words do creep strange ways –

The Certainty

the radiant outskirts
of the land which is real
gleam forth –
in the land which is real
I have my friend –
there we shall touch
the simple nakedness
of each other –,
my friend and I –

four is the sacred number
in the land which is real –
my friend and his woman,
I and my woman,

in the holy grove
there are the four trees
of our common silence –

I have caught a glimpse
of the land which is real –
nothing
shall turn my pace –

Etching

lapwing crying
circle black
crying curve white
in the air—
saltmarsh turning
gray-green wet
with a closed egg
in the center—

ocean blushing sliding
into the sun fire,
evening breathing salt
toward morning's wind—
a gull vanishing in veiled rush,
fisherman wakes to day—

P.B.

Fishing Hamlet

october's horizon
is higher than the church spire—
on its jagged edge
small steamers wander
single file—
against the coast the sea beats black
drumming—
and tall weatherbeaten men
split kindling
with small axes—

N.C. & E.H.

Winter

storms rumble—
winter wages its war—
the ocean wanders
along the coasts—
the sky follows it
high overhead—
small houses cower
in fear against the ground—
the moon's icy eye
stares through the wall of night
on men gathering coal

N.C. & E.H.

March

snow lies
firm and white—
the sea shines
summer blue—
flaming sun
and ice-clear air
burn in tired eyes—
seabirds mate,
hoarse starlings shriek—
night comes
black and deep—
boats follow
shoaling herring—
over the land to the west
a star sparkles green—

P.B.

Tove Meyer
(1913–1972)

TOVE MEYER was one of the few female poets of the inter-war period who radically transformed poetic language in a fusion of expressionism and imagism.

She published *Guds Palet* (God's Palette) 1935, *Efter Regn* (After Rain) 1940, *I en Have Derhjemme* (In a Garden Back Home) 1953, and *Havoffer* (Sea Sacrifice) 1961.

In a Garden back Home

In a garden back home, before time was time—
The days were high and came from afar,
rocking like camels through my ever-blue oasis,
where the yellow gravel was wet and nagging beneath me,
where the round scents went incessantly through me,
like gentle swords,
and the flowers buzzed like fireflies around my hands.

Small, conical and tough, I could not sing
but was often alone with invisible others, small,
tough and conical like myself.
Oh, how we ate under the hogweed—that moontree:
Purple snails, angelic fat and the hides of jaguars,
drinking drum-ale
or we rode on tempestuous elderbush horses,
chasing hosts of raging red-headed swaggering turkeys.

And under the evening's magic cloak, when the sun flowed
down there along the ground, we were many little ones

who danced in a ring or back and forth,
back and forth in a constant rocking rhythm:
There came three men across the sea—across the sea—
—aye—whatalie—whatalasie—who—
Until all the king's sons and daughters floated away,
up under towers and roofs in chambers of gold
beneath feathery mountains· of red-robin clouds.

Sleep was listening alert to the wandering waters,
panther-forests creeping over lonely roads,
the sea's distant sirens were giant teddy bears
standing erect, droning out nasal sounds to
the moon's astonished jaws
and walking away with mammoth steps.
Till at length all those white fountains sprang forth
from a flower at my ear, and the baker's golden loaves
almost burst in the bag
on the dewy doorstep.

In a garden back home before time was time.

Farther on, I was jumping, my bottom in tight pants
across the tarred roofs, cherry-red and cheerful
with tons of pits in my stomach
—that could grow into trees—
And farther on, we were many with caps and hats, belts and
          daggers,
who crossed the prairie, discovered fire
and roasted bloody buffalo meat.
Often for days and weeks we did not forget the fire
—but sniffed and gulped down the smoke
which stuck in our tanned flesh.

Those were the days of my boyhood, before I became a girl.
My mother was the only one in the world with a chignon at
          her neck.

She stepped with dignity and lavishly as a queen
scooped out the brown beans there in the white house
under the crown of the acacia, where no one came,
—only the nuthatch pecking boats out of nuts—
and the sun was always stuck in the great fork above
boiling with pent-up anger
at noon.

Then it was lovely to be a girl and in the evening stand in
        the swing
and sail gently backwards and see the stars come from without
and swing in under the moon's rolling wheel,
see Mars go down and Venus rise
and Orion topple over his sword, while the Great Bear
was reeling toward the horizon
and wait
wait for the sound of a door, his footsteps on the lane
and jump down and let the knife
sing its way into the post with the sign
which read: Cherry La—

Oh, when at last we were sitting in our own trees, which were
        blowing, blowing
and singing a clumsy song
stronger than light
drowning out the falling stars.

In a garden back home, before time was time.

Home is no longer home, and the days have shrunk.
I stand again by a fence, but now it is rusty.
The garden is no garden and knows me not.
No longer can anyone walk here, who never knew the days of
        the camel rides—
and who will see again
from the little hole in the fence
the clouds' high hats wandering over the fields?

Alas, days are days!

I will crumple my old hat and depart from the place of death,
without a look over my shoulder (as I did then),
thoughtlessly and filled with longing
to step into Reason's
endless, flat-shoed, scentless-stinking funeral procession.

Farewell, then, to you, my wing-eyed friends!

                                                    L.T.

Tove Ditlevsen
(1918–1975)

TOVE DITLEVSEN grew up in a working-class district in Copenhagen. She published her first volume of poems at an early age (1939) and has since then published a large number of collections of poems, short stories, and novels which have reached an unusually large public, owing to the author's shrewdness and experience as well as an extraordinary knack of straightforward and subtle expression.

She has also published three volumes of controversial memoirs.

Sunday

Nothing ever happens on a Sunday.
You never meet a new love
on a Sunday.
It is the Day of the Distressed.
Boarding-house day or family day.
The woman's most painful hours
when she pictures her lover
with his babies on his knee
while his wife, smiling,
walks in and out with tempting trays.
An accursed day.

Once everything must have been different.
Why else should we all of us
look forward to Sunday all week?
When we went to school, perhaps?
But even then the church bells sounded

sorrowful and gray like rain and death.
Even then the voices of the grownups
were weak and toneless as if they fumbled
for Sunday words in vain.

The smell of mould and old bread,
of sleep, rubber boots, and chicory
rose up even then through the stairway,
and the street, stiff, empty, and different
in a desolate way—
the smell of Sunday crammed us
with a fat layer of that disappointment
which follows an expectation
without a particular aim.

But when, then? Somewhere before memory
there was a happiness, an irresistible expectation,
which no one could yet disappoint.
Then the church bells meant that Father was home,
the moustache, the dark eyebrows, and the smell of snuff
was there and stayed there, somewhere near,
and perhaps your young mother's laughter
sounded more merry than on all the other days.

It is Sunday. You never meet
a new love on a Sunday.
You sit in the parlor
rigid and flat like a cardboard figure
in the eyes of the children.
They scrape with their feet
and quarrel listlessly with each other.
"We ought to do something," you say.
"Yes," comes a voice from behind the paper.
Then you both fall silent because everything you feel
like doing is hidden and secret
and would be unacceptable to the other.

The church bells are ringing.
The nostrils of the children
are filled with a hopeless, inherited smell.
Across their sweet faces moves
a temporary ugliness.
A faded light
is growing in their eyes.

But we all look forward to Sunday
all week, all our lives,
look forward to hundreds
of futile, exhausting, long Sundays.
Family day, boarding-house day,
the hell of secret lovers. ‑
That day when the nauseating grayness of the grownups
seeps into the children and decides
the incomprehensible Sunday gloom of years to come.

K.M.

Divorce 1

He would
in the case of a divorce
demand half
of everything
he said.
Half a sofa
half a television
half a summerhouse
half a pound of butter
half a child.

The apartment was his
he said
because it was in his name.

The point was
that he loved her.

She loved someone
whose wife would
demand half
of everything.

That was in the marriage law.
It was as clear
as two and two are four.

The lawyer said
that it was right.

She smashed up half
of everything
and tore the tax sheet in pieces.
Then she went out
to the Home for Women on Jagtvej
with half a child.

The child was teased at school
because he only had
one ear.
Otherwise life could be
put up with in that way
since it could not be
otherwise.

                                        A.F.

You Who Someone

You who someone
is still fond of
you who want to be loved
you, the receiving one—
how little you understand
of what was never yours:

I collect
windfall fruits
from the hanging gardens
of my heart
I cushion the fall
I do not want to be loved—
I hide Kaspar Hauser
the man without a past,
of royal descent,
from those who have designs
on his life—
I teach him the language
and the use of arms
with a patience that
before the metamorphosis
was alien to me,
I teach myself
to love
and to avoid
the dangerous love of the loved ones
which will make
the placidly growing
plants wither
in the sheltering garden
of my heart.

                                        K.M.

The Round Room

Expanded to breaking point
branching off without control
insurmountably tangled up
like a pregnancy forced upon me,
I wonder whether all this
was really necessary?
Couldn't one have made do
with incredibly little,
the detail of a detail
practically nothing
something like a tin
whose lid fits and
slips silently on
in this world
of shoddy workmanship.

Everything whole
is too overwhelming
a whole person
is impossible to cope with,
unlikely, unbearable.
All those nuts and bolts
loose or missing
and the stock of spares
was spent already in childhood.
Angry mechanics who already
while learning the trade ran away
eye me with suspicion and think
I want to cut down
just to hurt them.

Everything clinks and clanks
and falls apart—

Children rushed through me
as if through a chute
fat, bleeding, and flabby,
I gave up finding the flaw
and the repairmen
were late.

Weariness flows through my veins
I, used up so soon, in whose house
strange people lie
in beds just botchedly joined together
which must be constantly changed for new ones
where the footboard is missing
so they can grow
unimpeded
in their sleep.

With supreme effort
I pick a hole in the
fetal membrane
of my unwanted life.
A splashing sound
fills all the world.
We're cutting down
I tell my nosy neighbor
and then withdraw
to a perfectly round room
with the only thing necessary with me:
a tin whose lid fits
and to my infinite delight
slips on without a sound
in the unbroken silence
I have longed for all my life.

                                        K.H.

Divorce 3

It is not easy
to be alone
other people
have impatient
waiting-room eyes.
The floor pulls
your steps away
underneath you.
You move
hand over hand
from hour to hour.
A vocabulary
of around
a hundred words
was not included
in the division of the household.

The craving for
something annoying
the lack of
strong smells.
Cold smoke
in the curtains.
The bed is
too wide now.
Girl friends leave
at potato-boiling time.

Freedom
comes first
with the next train
an unknown

traveler
who doesn't
like children.

The dog is
uneasy
sniffs at
the wrong pants legs
is soon
in heat.

You read books
watch television
take in
nothing
are suddenly
very happy
in the morning
and in despair
before evening.

It's a transition
girl friends say
something you have
to go through.
Weightless as an
astronaut
you float around
in empty rooms
and wait
for the freedom
to do
what you
no longer
want to do.

                                          A.F.

Self-Portrait 1

I can not:
cook
wear a hat
make people comfortable
wear jewelry
arrange flowers
remember appointments
thank others for gifts
tip correctly
keep a man
show interest
at meetings for parents.

I can not
stop:
smoking
drinking
eating chocolate
stealing umbrellas
oversleeping
forgetting to remember
birthdays
and to clean my nails.
Telling people what they
want to hear
giving away secrets
liking
strange places
and psychopaths.

I can:
be alone

wash dishes
read books
form sentences
listen
and be happy
without guilt feelings.
A.F.

Self-Portrait 4

There lives in
my childhood street
an old woman
who remembers me
when I was young.
I was wild
she says
the whole house shook
when I took the stairs
in leaps from the fourth floor.

That picture of me
is disturbing
and pushes itself
in front of my own
as when photos
are superimposed
one over the other.

I fear
the place I have
in the memory of others.
They remind me of things
I myself have forgot.
They have stolen

my face
before it was
used up
they set it often
outside their own.

I do not remember
my childhood
old woman
the grownups were
all alike and
without age.
She has a knowledge
of me she doesn't disclose
a secret I never
have told.

It fills her and
keeps death away
she lies and intends
to outlive me.
I certainly never took
the stairs in long leaps
I was a quiet child
I loathe her.

                                   A.F.

Piet Hein
(1905)

PIET HEIN has since the beginning of the forties published several collections of his much-loved *Gruk* and has lately recreated selections of them in English as *Grooks*.

He has published cartoons in the *Saturday Review of Literature*.

He has made numerous scientific inventions, among others the super-ellipse. He is *Doctor honoris causa* of Yale University, 1972.

In addition to the *Grooks* he has published essays and poems of which many have been published in English.

Hamlet Anno Domini

Our Destiny lies dormant
    in our dreams
Our future is
    such stuff as dreams are made of?
The task will take
    the toil of loyal teams.
So may you be such men
    as teams are made of!

This World 'of mutual dependence
    gives
Us truly Hamlet's
    two alternatives
Though in a modern version — :
    Coexistence
    or no existence.

Majority Rule

His party was the Brotherhood of Brothers,
and there were more of them than of the others.
That is, they constituted that minority
which formed the greater part of the majority.
Within the party, he was of the faction
that was supported by the greater fraction.
And in each group, within each group, he sought
the group that could command the most support.
The final group had finally elected
a triumvirate whom they all respected.
Now of these three, two had the final word,
because the two could overrule the third.
One of these two was relatively weak,
so one alone stood at the final peak.
He was: THE GREATER NUMBER of the pair
which formed the most part of the three that were
elected by the most of those whose boast
it was to represent the most of most
of most of most of the entire state—
or of the most of it at any rate.
He never gave himself a moment's slumber
but sought the welfare of the greatest number.

And all the people, everywhere they went,
knew to their cost exactly what it meant
to be dictated to by the majority.
But that meant nothing,—they were the minority.

The Me above the Me

Giving in is no defeat.
Passing on is no retreat.
Selves are made to rise above.
You shall live in what you love.

The Common Well
To Charles Chaplin

The well you invite us to drink of
is one that no drop may be bought of.
You think of what all of us think of
but nobody else could have thought of.

Losing Face

The noble art of losing face
may one day save the human race
    and turn into eternal merit
what weaker minds would call disgrace.

The Road to Wisdom

The road to wisdom?—Well, it's plain
and simple to express:
       Err
       and err
       and err again
       but less
       and less
       and less.

Hint and Suggestion
Admonitory Grook Addressed to Youth.

The human spirit sublimates
the impulses it thwarts;
a healthy sex life mitigates
the lust for other sports.

The True Defence

The only defence
that is more than pretence
    is to act on the fact
that there is no defence.

Consolation Grook

Losing one glove
is certainly painful,
but nothing
    compared to the pain
of losing one,
throwing away the other,
and finding
    the first one again.
        Written in English

Halfdan Rasmussen
(1915)

HALFDAN RASMUSSEN was of Copenhagen working-class origin. He contributed to Syndicalist and Socialist newspapers and underground publications during the German occupation.

He has written children's books and an entirely personal humorous verse genre, *Tosserier* (Nonsenses), a selection of which has been published in English in 1973 under the title *Halfdane's Sense and Nonsense*.

His chief volumes of poems are: *Soldat eller menneske* (Soldier or Man) 1941, *Digte under Besættelsen* (Poems during the Occupation) 1945, *På Knæ for livet* (Kneeling before Life) 1948, *Forventning* (Expectation) 1951, and *Stilheden* (Silence) 1962.

Sardine

I did dream once of getting out. The bottom
one out of six all headless brothers
the other five constantly reassured me
that a tin is safer for little fish.

Thinking of many peculiar things, I told
tales and fables for the others.
Sang of the sea and the shoal of stars
in the milky way in the sky.

Wake them? I could not do it. They all
slept so soundly, greased in oil,
quite content with this state of affairs,
all's well in this tin world order.

104

Dreamt that Saint Sebastian would come
from morning mists of the Atlantic
and free all the small sardines of this world
with his can opener shining like gold.

I longed for the deep sea but was pressed
to a nice conformist sardine whose spine
little by little looked like all the others
soft and limp like a stillborn lug. ‑

Never dream of the sea any more. Have now
silently accepted this tin church of mine
where I rest in peace among my brothers
awaiting the Unction, the last of the oil.

K.H.

Something about Heroes

Life is like a morning present
and the soul a pilgrim's cheer.
Crocuses are blue and pleasant,
while I have my morning beer. ‑
High above, a lark suspended
like a far-off, feathered seed.
Have a lark! For who intended
us to do heroic deed?

This is rural, nice and quiet,
I can't hear the madding crowd,
I have roots in peace—no riot,
I grow parsley and feel proud.
Let the world go round its bend
or amok or mad and fight,
I'll agree with foe and friend
and myself, and be allright.

Lots of people join in planning
how to blow the world from hence.
All such skirmishes I'm banning,
I am King within my fence.
They have Russian pacts and Natos
so the earth can't be at rest.
Earthing up my own potatoes
I can feel unearthly blest.

I will not plant blows on noses,
I may sow, but never mines.
All my thorns are on the roses,
I'm a sage with columbines.
With my paltry sum of money
I can make the two ends meet,
I can send my wife, my honey,
walking gardenpaths, not streets.

Carrots, cabbage, cress is found in
beds with beans in files and ranks.
Cheques are met on my account in
my own vegetable banks.
When the surface seems to harden
and my spade I "cannot" find,
then my mole may dig the garden,
which he doesn't seem to mind.

Nelson's battles are historic,
Samson pulled the temple down,
I'm no hero, I am Yorick,
on the stage of life I'm clown.
I have never been a Samson,
I can see with either eye.
Willingly I pay my ransom;
cowards live when heroes die.

Time may pass, while Time's recruiting
men from lists for heroes' jobs.
Un-enlisted, loathing shooting
this poor poet softly sobs.
Cow'ring coward, keep your head low!
Just a scratch can make me sore.
I would rather reap my meadow
than reap honor in a war.

What's the use of all this beating?
Why use swearwords when we meet?
I'll shake hands with all when greeting.
I'm the beatnik who won't beat.
Let them lash at one another,
those who're strong and stern and tough.
I'll sing songs as taught by Mother,
I have not yet had enough.

Life is still a lovely present,
Earth is still a lovely earth.
I'm now full of beer—that's pleasant,
I know flowers and their worth.
When the wars get epidemic
and they ask us all to shoot, ⬋
I'll compose a peaceful epic
where the blood is just beetroot.

                               K.H.

Old Johnson, the Letterbox-painter

Old Johnson, the letterbox-painter,
got caught in the box and grew fainter,
it squeezed and he sneezed so the letters
were scattered from Glasgow to Cheddars.

Spinsterly, longing Camilla,
who sat all alone in her villa,
and had her fifth cup and some mutton,
was popular all of a sudden.

Ten thousand letters from Adams
and more from French messieurs and madams,
a postcard with snow right from Norway,
and income-tax forms in the doorway.

K.H.

Snowman Frost and Lady Thaw

Snowman Frost and Lady Thaw
went for walks and thought of more,
found a garden seat and sat,
talked of love and this and that.

Snowman Frost, a little weak,
asked her, "May I kiss your cheek?"
But as Lady Thaw was hot,
all she got was a wet spot.

As their passion rose in heat,
off he melted from the seat,
when he kissed her tender lips,
he slipped through her fingertips.

All alone without "amore"
on the seat sits Lady Thaw.
Snowman Frost no more will hug,
she must keep him in a mug.

                                        K.H.

Morten Nielsen
(1922–1944)

MORTEN NIELSEN studied comparative literature before he was killed as a member of the Danish Resistance Movement.

He was a contributor to the underground anthology *Der Brænder en Ild* (A Fire Is Burning), 1944. His 'intensely existential' poetry was of great importance to his generation.

His collections of poems are *Krigere Uden Vaaben* (Warriors Without Arms) 1943, and *Efterladte digte* (Posthumous Poems) 1945. Two editions of his letters have been published in 1962 and 1966.

We're Sending Dance Music at Night

I am the glow of the cigarette
and the rhythm of the jazz,
fast, light, but with an undertone
of death.

I am restaurant premises
and dancing floors
—an echo of the dance that's on there,
slow but with an undertone
          of the rhythm of creations,
hard and hot and mute.

I am the gust of fire
in your nerves—
the barren intention of day and night
in sending you down the road
you're lost on.

110

I am the rhythm of myself—
cheerful—without happiness—
            hard and hot and mute.
Never more the white
trembling rhythm¹ of a flower opening.

Not the rhythmic play of earth
or the song through the wheat,
not the rhythm by which spring
is unfolded
and created.

Not the good
rhythm of the globe, of growth close and gentle,
            and eternally great and strict.
—I am the rhythm and refrain
of the dancing tunes of Hunger, Time and Death.

                                                        P.B.

Announcement of a Defeat

I am standing on a couch talking a strange drunken drivel.
I am proposing the art of prophecy to a forum of beer and
            tobacco.
I am saying just one sentence. We're just two who understand it.
I say: Go to hell in blessed spring.

Oh, if you knew how good spring was once.
Chalkwhite boughs were stretched-out lines of verse, chalkwhite
            on blue.
By day and by night my enormous heart of smarting joy
had a door wide open to every refraction of light and every
            small sound.

I'm abundantly drunk and understand nothing and still I
 remember it all.
I betray a spring, for the meaning of spring in me fell into decay.
I propose my will: One spring must be emptied like bottles
 and smashed.
I deliver *my* Sermon on the Mount here. And we're two who
 understand it.

P.B.

I See Tonight

I see tonight his outstretched hand
is ready to separate
calmly Spirit and Dust.
A cut and a few drops of blood drop by drop
—sink and disappear
into the peace of the Great Sleep.

Nothing is lost. None have called.
Lie quiet—a sigh—
all is done,
what happened to you and is going to happen.
It is snowing darkness now
and growing calm with snow.

— There's a whisper in your heart, disturbing and hot:
You betray too much,
you brought me too little.
Then a whisper of fear: Unfulfilled, forsaken
your fate is left behind
if you go tonight.

—You must grow and bloom and put forth your seed.
You are still too low to die.

P.B.

We Couldn't Stay away from Each Other

Your skin, it's fragrant as a meadow. And your feet,
I turned them for a second toward my heart
and did not know myself what that meant—:
You shall walk on me now, gently as light.
—And we cannot stay away from each other.
You are lying silently in front of me, stretched and curving.
But your skin—white, with a glow of darkness in it—
responds to what whispers in *my* skin—

... Receives me now, trembles as if fingers
had stroked the heart—your fingers
want to find my heart—and search for it and forget—
So light is everything, freed like a childhood—
the pale window, the glow from you—
We scarcely talk to each other
but our hands never rest alone.

You receive me, let me go, receive me,
and my lips are stroking your shoulders...

And we cannot stay away from each other.
I am so filled with this truthful beauty
blazing purely like rainlight all night....
I whisper with my mouth close over yours:

You are as beautiful as your eyes—

P.B.

They Are Playing Ball on the Road

The air is June-like and clear and tender,
and the flying ball jumps up to the hem of your dress,
and you throw again, and I hear a bat striking—
And across the hedge the sky is eternally blue.

You throw again. And you bend a little while throwing.
A trembling through your shoulders nails you to
a hidden revelation. I stand here knowing more than you.
The tenderest rhythm of the world
is striking you now.

Have I myself been turned toward other things for years,
Have I traded more precious things and abandoned them all,
and am I a boy of twelve or twenty-one?
—Summer is coming, and the ball shall fly and fly—

                                                        P.B.

Ole Sarvig
(1921)

OLE SARVIG is a poet, novelist, playwright, and a critic of
art. He has written about 'the Cobra Movement' and Edvard
Munch (*Edvard Munchs Grafik* [The Graphic Art of Edvard
Munch]) 1948, and has adapted four of Shakespeare's plays
into Danish.

His contribution to modern poetry describes a gradually ris-
ing consciousness: cognition is not a priori, before language, it
is born within language.

Grønne digte (Green Poems) 1943, *Jeghuset* (The I-House)
1944, *Mangfoldighed* (Multitude) 1945, *Legende* (Legend) 1946,
and *Menneske* (Man) 1948.

He has traveled widely and lived for long periods in various
European countries. Several of his novels have been translated
into a number of languages, among others *Stenrosen* (The Stone
Rose) 1955, *De Sovende* (The Sleepers) 1958, *Havet Under
mit vindue* (The Sea Below My Window) 1960, *Limbo* (Limbo)
1963, and *Glem ikke* (Don't Forget) 1972.

My Sorrow

The strange old villa of my sorrow
with cold verandas to the north
and useless tower-rooms.

Always in the shadow
of the dark green garden of pines,
overgrown, forgotten,
shunned by everyone.

115

There often I walk alone
in echoing rooms of the damp
in the mouldy silence,
broken only by the insect people's
scraping on the walls,

—these small crunching creatures
who in a hundred years
will have lived the house to ashes.

                              O.S./A.T.

Pale Morning

Always I hear Truth shout his wares
among the houses.
But when I open the window
the peddler has vanished with his cart,
and the houses huddle there with the usual faces,
their wan sun-smiles,
in a day like all the others.

Came the great morning.
Huge lights blazed in space.
Faint bright colors
shivering in the chill.
Truth dinned at my ear
and was off to other streets,
many roofs away,
where now others hear him calling.

                              O.S./A.T.

Walk

Coming from the misty dream-plains
I pass through word-forests.

Here from high places often
I look back on the plains,
but branches cast shadows, and everything grows distant,
and I am on the way
to the big mountain of the sea:
its shimmering forest lakes,
on whose banks I often sit,
are stones, blasted away and carried
once from the mountain's country.

And I am on my way again
walking through the dark of the forest,
where many beautiful old trees
have died in the night frost
in these regions.

And on all sides
hosts of tall dark nettles blooming.

O.S./A.T.

Skylights

The clouds, the ships, huge, black,
these gray navies
sail past out there.

And I stand here at the window
beside my flowers,
which reach for the light
and climb behind the glass.

— — —

So are they all,
artists, painters,
creepers under skylights.

Some never blossom.
Some have beautiful flowers.

O.S./A.T.

Thought-stillness
(For Giorgio Chirico)

There behind the city's banks—
the empty square behind those temples—
the soul goes, calling.

A street vanishes into the horizon.

And heavy black shadows fall
as the sun scorches life
into white unreality.

— — —

People walk like distant dots
crossing streets
and along the edges of the vacant square
of anticipation.

A war lurks over there
beyond the rooftops.

And thought is mute
on its tower.

O.S./A.T.

The Moon's Day

The moon's day
shines in the earthly night
hushing desolate houses,
sharp blue strips of light between them.

It is night over the world
and in the furnaces of the stars.

Like the spark of a dream
or an event long awake
in the white backyard of the moon
or the flaming street of the sun.
The metered light ticks away on the stairs
where doors bang,—and in a minute stops,
while fates come home late
to where they live.

The huge midnight stars
hang fresh as dew
in heavy bunches, like white flowers
against the ice-pane.

Tomorrow—is unborn and black.

O.S./A.T.

Christ in the Grain Fields

Tonight I saw the grain,
the dreaming grain,
the grain and husks of all the living,
here in these fields.

I saw it this morning about five—
pale hour when Christ came,
when children are born,
when fires break out.

It was so beautiful. Sleepers so hushed. Calm.
Christ moved like a moon through the grain.

O.S./A.T.

Thistles

Thistle-fleets ride in all oceans
rule the boundless gray.
Thistle-forests drift over the sea
detonating, flashing fire.

Some die now
in these very hours,
drops boiling away . . .

— — —

But smoke hides the thistle-coast,
muffles
scream of sun deep inland.

O.S./A.T.

Overlooking the Cemetery
For Per Nørgaard, the composer

Often the apartments were empty
across the street from the cemetery:

People have fled—out of the huge windows,
into the dazzling space,
filed past, singing to the grave,
roamed away over the fences
of that green wilderness,
trampling them down.

But the willows kneel. Neck by neck,
green.

Many moved into those rooms.
Just in these last few years.
Motors and horses hauled their furniture.

Out there the light still blinding:
Soon. Soon we'll come.

But the plants have shadow-houses
in the midst of day.
Leafy eaves.

O.S./A.T.

R^4

And the men went away
forgetting everything
behind them, above them—
remembering only themselves.

For many days,
in the long streets' corridors,
in sleeping, in waking
in the chain of days,
in the void of light,
in white overalls.

Searching,
Found one day
a tiny white gate,
opened it:
God was there,
and the abyss,
seething empty,
loudly inviting.

Again they close the cupboard
betraying nothing,
proceed as before,
doomed,
burning
deep within.

O.S./A.T.

Jørgen Nash
(1920)

JØRGEN NASH is a painter, poet, and organizer of happenings. He was a member of the central committee of the International Situationists, Paris 1959–62. He was also editor and publisher of the underground magazine *Drakabygget* (Bauhaus-situationists), which is also the name of the International commune of situationists in Sweden, a center of various art activities.

Among his collections of poems are *Atom Elegien* (The Atom Elegy) 1946, *Vredens sange* (Songs of Wrath) 1951, *Solen* (The Sun) 1956, and together with his brother Asger Jorn: *Stavrim og sonetter* (Alliterations and Sonnets) 1960, *Det naturlige smil* (The Natural Smile) 1965, *I denne transistorsommer Eller dagen H.* (In This Transistor Summer or the Day H.) 1967, and *Sweden and their immigrants* (Stockholm 1975).

He has also published essays, two novels, and translations of works by Dylan Thomas and Jacques Prévert.

Song of Silence

Be quiet, be quiet, open your eyes. Listen to me without questioning answers. I am catching memories. I am catching melodies. On a green bough the nightingale is singing.

Walk softly, walk softly. I am touching a round stone, which in millions of years has been shone on by the moon and by tens of thousands of winking stars and by the days and the sun-embers of dawn.—Be quiet. It feels as though the stone is stroking me under my twenty-five-year old palms. The rainbow-shining songs of earth are my joy.

124

Walk softly, be quiet, open your eyes. Sunblind are the rain pearls of dew, and over the red lilies of my heart space is filled with the buzzing of bees. Perhaps, perhaps I shall never find my fluttering birds.

P.B.

Let Us Sing of the Paradise Earth

Let us sing of the paradise earth,
the indomitable movements, the trembling song of the eyes.
We liberate summer's fragrant hives, its soul.
We annul the sea's Fimbul winter, its martyrdom.
We sow spring flowers so everyone can exclaim: Look,
the petals are growing in the horizon of vibrations.
Yes, we have all been born in the pounding heart,
and the tidal wave will bring us new health.

You who perpetually mock the seeker of drowning
with the municipal lifebelt,
I pray you: Lay your ear to the green cheek of the grass
and listen to the redeeming heavenly rhythm of the showers.
For it is in the air, in the universe and in you:
the days are the meek sprinters of the seasons.
Only get your close-up of time's nervous system.
Still the sun will spread its softening light.

On the taut violin strings of the highroads
the migrant birds sit in pairs and listen to the wind's string band
and let their blinking eyes suck up a cosmic view.
O sister of the salt of life—your tender love
is the skylark of the pearly dreams of the stamens.
That is the process. That is the leap. That is the moment.
The furrows of love warming the moles,
and human rejoicings, reunion here consummated.

To love the ticklish brows of butterflies,
to be two bodies of lust rolling
in the microscopic crystals of the snow
so the world shall not keep on blushing.
Male and female animals shall lick their mouths.
All motives are again and again the same arabesque,
for the whole carries forth victoriously the enrichment of life.
Sensual in all situations.

But at the pessimists' wailing wall the friends
of the world-famous grape philosophy of the fox
must elect pain's escape artists saints
and prefer happiness with feet of clay,
every time the Messiah is overwhelmed with gurgling organ notes,
so hail to the godly gapers' feast,
for soon we shall see through the stars
singing of the myriad-souled reality.

Hail to the aorta of the poetry of earth
which alone can thaw the smile of frost
and the death of the figures of fire.
Hail to the humans who devotedly drink
from time's communicating vessels.
Hail to the eternal cycle of spirit and seasons,
work, rest, play, seriousness, day and night.
Earth will be kissed to a richer life.

P.B.

dreams come true sometimes

(»here thou incestous murderous damned dane«)

hamlet

Try for a miracle
one sunny day
earthmovers
our cat is transatlantic in both directions

HAMLETIZATION

the white democratic cat is important
and we continue
        sleeping
beneath mink blankets
small enough to be nimble in city traffic
        economical in fuel demands
everybody is doing it
times change, but some things remain unaltered
our white atomic cat for instance

she loved the man who gave it to her too

World Youth

Bird Song

Di ver ti men to

Tii tii tii tii tii

sissississ

ity tvity tvittvevéy -øsis siss-øsi ss -is si ss - øsissitt

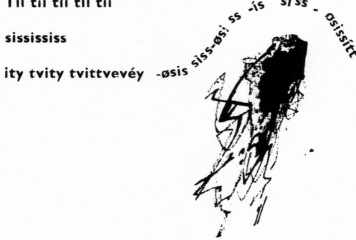

Some People Don't Like Bacon

Bundgård Povlsen
(1918)

BUNDGÅRD POVLSEN was born in Copenhagen; he was trained as a blacksmith, and for some years was a journalist with various provincial newspapers.

Among his collections of poems are *Hverdagsdigte* (Everyday Poems) 1953, *Mur og rum* (Wall and Space) 1962, *Tidsdigte* (Poems of Time) 1967, *Flammekrebsen* (The Flaming Crayfish) 1971, and *Dag/lig/dag* (Dai/ly/Day) 1974.

Month of August Poem

Forever the river of crushed plums
through heavy gardens streaming with mould
through dark chambers that stream with mould.
Forever in this life an August
with night like an oozing rain
cooling the blushing fruit of late summer
and the childmother's ember under ashes of pain.
Forever August forever
forever twisted iron bars'
morning of havoc, blackened metal.
August with the splintered stones
down to the river of crushed plums.
Forever this life the life of the lovers ✸
and the child's astounded August
with the cracked walls and collapsed mortar
and with the shadows' destruction like stalks
elegiacally creeping through uncounted shafts
and children mad with joy suddenly burning ➛

131

and a live hare losing its skin like a cloak
and a blind mouse between rusty razor blades.
Who can endure August in his life
with the creeping shadows
over the crushed life's river
from April to August
after which the metal will melt
in your eyes
and why shouldn't metal and iron
➡seek orgasm
like the flowers in the eyes of my beloved
and what happened in the black
hole of war in the wall? August
eternal river of debasement
with the mournful lofty tolling of bells
vibrating like cracks in walls
and like the nostrils of horses on the clay slope,
like the screaming metal of spotlights
➡ and like the trembling of sudden calm. August
—yes, my August throwing ring upon ring of unrest
beyond the walls to the shadow-heap of heroes,
to the matting of fates
along the river of crushed plums
toward piles of death
through the gutters
through the vulnerable pipes of wires in the abdomen
through the whole system from whose center
a child's smile is spreading.
Deep under this the river of crushed plums
(and actually it is an autumn in our gardens)
which has also colored this day's sky
yellow in the horizon and darkly frayed;
it might be the houses, the gardens of childhood
with a clammy rose dangling from the gate.

           P.B.

Love Poem

My love has become homeless
owns no roof over its head
now when I know it far too well.
Now I know that love
is not for house and home.
Love is homeless
Love is where you do
its bidding when you leave
your house and home, safety
is not for love.

To love is a quick death.

To grow old is to remember
your death for a long time.

P.B.

Lizard

The beginning of a lizard
almost always becomes: Lizard.

The lizard rather easily reaches
the result: Lizard.

The beginning of a lizard
almost never becomes a sparrow.

In this way most beings become
their own sort of lizards from the beginning.

Once when I was a human being
quick as lightning I saw a lizard.

P.B.

My Black Windows Shining Miles away in the Night

Going out
to receive them
family or criminals
in the rain this dark night
I keep the lights on
in the house I leave
and where we shall gather
if I find them
in the dark—my window
looking black from inside
shines far out here,
now in the night,
and I see it
and I am thinking:
could they have come?

P.B.

The Blue Coffee Pot

There's a thing you don't understand
but you must:
My mother's blue coffee pot
at five in the morning
against the yellow sun,
and a bit of coffee grounds:
Earth
and the blue sky.

P.B.

Patience among Trees

The trees do not follow
their leaves up
and fly away from Denmark.
Most birds do
who inhabit the trees of Denmark
in summertime; but now
when it's December
the trees are dressed in bark,
the birch for instance
the beech for instance and the spruce and the fir,
the white bark, the gray bark, the brown
watched by me and the blackbird
the flying blackbird
kicking the leaves
when it lands
in there among the trees
in my sight spreading out in Denmark.

I'm sitting here
with my ass cold
leaning my back and the rest of me
against a woodpile
expecting mice, birds, friends.
I'm a patient type.

P.B.

A Superannuated Romantic

Now I've stared
at girls and at stars
and I don't care to see them anymore.
They're all so damned alike
inside and out
especially the girls. Only their tits
are differently placed.
I'm tired, too
of books and boxing fights
to say nothing of bottom fights
and woods at twilight
and all that crap about flesh.
You should love everybody, oh yeah,
I've had enough of all this
"through the many to the one"
and of this talk about the one and only.
I sit down at midnight
lonely with the bottle and the glass
just like my dead friend
August Strindberg, "The Bondwoman's Son"
and crumple some blank sheets of paper.
They're lying there on the floor, then,
trembling slightly in convulsions,
I stare at that, totally drained.
By God, they've done well!
the girls from whom I expected
so much, really.
Now I give the crumpled paper a kick
and throw my worn-out body
onto the bed
mumbling a goodnight to my big toe.

N.C./P.B.

Ole Wivel
(1921)

O LE WIVEL started his own publishing house in 1945 and became a managing director of Gyldendal in 1953. He was one of the editors of the literary magazine *Heretica* and has been a teacher in the Danish folk high school. Ever since the war he has taken an active part in the cultural and political debate.

He has published essays and literary studies as well as memoirs and several collections of poems. Among the latter are *I fiskens tegn* (In the Sign of the Fish) 1948, *Jævndøgnselegier* (Equinoctial Elegies) 1949, *Nike* (Nike) 1958, and *Gravskrifter* (Epitaphs) 1970.

The Cologne Cathedral

Automobiles speed by it.
Like a hammer blow of the past,
contrary to probability
and the law of perpetual evolution
it stands, scarred and splintered
between the streets.
A cliff furrowed with dreams
or better:
an antenna of the past
created to pick up the heavenly blessings
that we totally ignore.
We clatter at the bottom of it, move chairs,
sell postcards, shout perhaps
(as when one scratches a fingernail on a stone).
Should much rather tear it down,
blow it to pieces,
a useless symbol of inner conditions

137

which no one admits (shining arches that span
the space of silence). Insolent efforts
to escape the place where we obviously find ourselves
these frenzied minutes
and the morphine-high at the end.
Silence and striving in one,
rising toward that
which is impervious to analyses and proof.
And yet everyone knows
there are tones
inaudible to the ear.
(Tastebuds on the tongue are dulled
by tobacco and old age.)
The music plays above our heads
and what we see
are the empty, ingenious racks of the music stands.

N.C.

Holy Andrew's Barrow

The green lobes of the spring seed
ripple in the wind.
The lark twirls his lucky wheel
in the blue.
Zealand's fields
and the Great Belt
sink the glittering sides of ships
in the heat-haze of the horizon.

But you
madcap on your cross
under shed roof
wind-beaten God
yourself devoted to yourself:
Why right here where Fogy-Andrew
hung his hat on a sunbeam?

A.T.

The Repentant Magdalene of the Roadside

Standing with your 'bare defenseless' knees
in the wind and gray daylight
outside of Gedsted.
Having set out on casual
asphalt adventure
and ended up in Himmerland between
hard hands.
A little rat ran across the road,
a little swindler lay down between your sheets.
A young girl's faded dreams called to life
on a hard mattress.
And now the rain penetrating
your much too thin dress
unmissed sleepy girl friend.

A.T.

Stenild Cemetery

Unbelievable that the graves are cleared so quickly.
Scarcely rotted, the dead are shoveled away.
An entire old age home laid in the ground
not counting those who had an awkward fate
goodbye dear children—
risen now to a graveless life along
a dike of boulders.
Tombstones of granite and marble
iron crosses small wreaths of flowers
a broken column
the book open to the quote and
the glum greetings to a young girl
from the entire postal district.

The wind hoots over the bare fields.
A tractor clangs along the village street.
But another girl rides her bike
up toward the storm with her bag full
of women's magazines.

A.T.

To Poul Winther the Painter

The wind tumbles grains of sand over the edge of the dunes.
Small tracks appear in the dazzling hollow.
Sand drifts on the beach, piles up
in shadowy pointed shapes in back of boxes
balls cans stones and empty bottles.
Sand-drift over the dunes.
— Moon-drift on warm nights.

Children running in the plain
small girls playing ball.
Boys sheltered by sunwarm sides of houses
blowing clay pipes. Soap-bubbles. Rainbow-foam.
Up along the coast's stiffened dash of waves
a jet darts pursued by its own din.
The shadows move, the very earth
flies infinitely slowly
a grain of sand in the universe
rainbowsparkling on its planned course.

A.T.

Erik Knudsen
(1922)

E RIK KNUDSEN has been a primary-school teacher, later a folk-high-school teacher. He is a socialist and educationist whose polemic texts and whose contributions to the current debate have influenced young people on the left wing throughout the postwar decades. He has written revues, satires, and plays for the theater, television, and radio and taken an active part in the campaign against the American war in Vietnam.

Among his collections of poems are *Til en ukendt gud* (To an Unknown God) 1947, *Blomsten og sværdet* (The Flower and the Sword) 1949, and *Journal* (Journal) 1963, and also the satirical pieces *Madman og hans verden* (Madman and His World) 1967, and *Babylon marcherer* (Babylon Marches) 1970.

My Lundbye Ecstasy

I was not myself, I was Lundbye,
sat on my child's stool safe with nature,
alone and happy in the open air.
The low plains, the oceans of the sky
were sketched, and filled as little of the paper
as the shadow of a cloverleaf. And I
received eyes. Everything opened like doors.
I sketched it and wrote. I never wanted
the dream to fly away. I was stubborn.
I held it tightly. There I sat, twelve years old,
with the world like a dog at my feet.

A.T.

141

The Flower and the Sword

Go into the forest? No, I dare not go
There where the dream's green Jambool trees grow.
Listen to the birds! No, I dare not believe
Such pure tones.' Beauty drives me crazy,
And harmony rings cruelly in my ears.

Why should I seek the shadowy delusion
Where the sun sharpens its glittering lies
And the flower scarcely hides its scorn?

Goodbye French horn, woodruff, and well-water.
Goodbye our little picnic in the open air.

Now from the field the shouts and din of battle.
Out out where everything is naked day.
Where swords flash, and spears weave
The roof of heaven,
Where banners burn, where drums call
The bird from the nest.

Out there where the dawn of victory is fleeing
And defeat, in black majesty,
Stands firm.

                                                        A.T.

Non Scholae

Budding greens . . . and snow!
Daffodils, December lightning
Spring on earth, winter in heaven
strange and frightening!
Growth and madness, terror and grace
magnificent view protected by panes
which still show:
Budding greens . . . and showers of snow!

Then all of a sudden:
Clouds riding at anchor—a dripping hush
The day agape and vacantly staring
as if attacked by thoughts . . . a hush
– – –
—To live is to meet
every new day without experience
without fear; with open eyes
to catch the thousand possibilities ⁻
and choose just one
to live is to become
more and more the others
more and more oneself
courageous, cheerful
bound and free

I forget if you laughed
but remember your words:

—you're so sure!
– – –
Clouds on the alert
      awaiting the signal
but the sun hangs back

In my room the buzz of a solitary fly
courageous, cheerful
bound and free

—You're so sure!
— — —
That's right I'm sure
if I'm just keen
and have a script
on which I may lean.

Sure on the rostrum
with a throat full of words
A Message to youngsters in search of advice:
—To live is to act
as if one believes. I believe
in community because
common sense neutral zones
l'homme révolté UN
a little kindly flock
in spite of all and imagination

I believe in my scaffold
of mainly lies
I allow myself to believe
even when treading water
in your questioning eyes

—You're so sure!
— — —
          I'm as sure—you're quite right—
as the tick of a taxi by day and by night
as Cordon Bleu experts and antique brass
as a Home Guard facing enemy gas
as prophets of weather and teetotalism
and experienced novices in socialism.

Budding greens ... and showers of snow
Spring on earth and winter in heaven
Pyrotechnic display ⁻
                    both brutal and gently ironic
— — —
Then the peculiar pageant is over

I'm sailing along in my rocking chair
dizzy, flooded with sun and air
dispose and discard, heap up vast amounts,
and cheat to tally—they're my thoughts-accounts.

To live is to leave
hour upon hour, day after day
faithfully forget
calmly continue
further along
the beaten track
courageous, cheerful
bound and free

Why?
Because.

                              May 1957
                                  K.H.

The Representatives

They start their day with an egg or two
They have a soft spot for westerns
They collect sums for handicapped children
They converse with the successor to the throne
They stick Indian feathers in their hair
They sign the visitors' books
They recommend junket and yogurt
They speak on Flag Day
They relax reading crime if it's good
They sing little songs on the T.V.
They quote the Great of the Past
They go down for a pint at the local
They can cope with numerous irons in the fire
They find time for carnivals and campaigns
They sell Danish cheese
They understand the United States
They give the prizes at beauty contests
They commemorate victims of the last occupation
They bounce along on pogo sticks
They are deeply devoted at heart
They pat dogs
They blame the young
for not bothering to argue.

Bourgeois All at Sea

You're ashamed, you're fed up with
your rich fat white wide world,
exploitation, racism, genocide,
"freedom," "democracy" . . . you just loathe
it all. Good. Your bad conscience
is a sign of life. You're no burnt-out case
like the imperialistic gamblers and
their small agents with blind eyes. But
what do you do with your shame?
What do you use it for?

2
Your heart with the rebels
Your feet in the fat soil
Playboy
of the Revolution.

3
Forget you were born
white and rich
Was Marx proletarian?
Was Engels?
Lenin?
Brecht?
You too can do something
You too
can prove your solidarity
with the suppressed, and the rebellions
you must settle with yourself
you must settle with your class:
Desert.

                         K.H.

Lise Sørensen
(1926)

APART from being a praised poet, Lise Sørensen is also an appreciated essayist with the pattern of sex roles as a main subject.

The two books *Digternes damer* (The Poets' Ladies) 1964, and *Mands- og moderhjerte* (Man's Courage, Mother's Heart) 1969 deals with woman's role in art and reality.

Among her collections of poems are *Blæsten udenfor* (The Wind Outside) 1956, *Sommerdalen* (The Summer Valley) 1962, *Epistler* (Epistles) 1966, and *Tro dine øjne* (Believe Your Eyes) 1973.

Hold My Hand

Hold my hand
It's so dark here
And so cold
I'm burning
Hold my hand
I didn't mean it
It's a bit slippery
Soon you'll be well
What beautiful music
How ominous!
Hold my hand
It hurts so much
It lasts so long
Something went wrong
Hold your fingers
Very gently in mine—

Even here in bed
We must remember our hands
They remember everything
They know:
Wherever we are *they* will be
Like frightened brothers and sisters
Misled in the dark

                                        N.C.

In the Dark

My mother looks up at me
from the bed
and says Hello young lady
It was kind of you
Because now I don't think
my daughter will come—

And I explain to her
who I am
She almost believes it
Later we say
goodbye
Meet again
in the dark where no one can be seen

I keep a sharp lookout
in traffic
I am a strange lady
on the street
That was *that* visit.

                                        N.C.

Boy's Life

Where is the child
in these boys
Where is the boy
in these men
Where is the man
in these males?

Everyone took from them
what they could use
Which left only
the best in them
What use is *that*?

Where is the man
in these men?
Perhaps in the words of Lincoln
"As I would not
be a slave
neither would I
be a master."

N.C.

Our Don John
Where he is
is a good place to be
for our more fat-
laden tissues
No breasts
are neglected
No rumps lonely
Few thighs are allowed
to go by unnoticed

But keep him away from the body's
batlet
Protect him from the thumpings
filled with terrible memories
Watch that he does not
fall asleep
with his ear toward your heart
or a finger
on your pulse
For then you will see him
leap in fright
as if from a time bomb

                        N.C.

Previously Unpublished

Permit me although I do not have any
connections to send herewith this no-
vel which I have entitled "The Gos-
sip Bench" It is about both my own
and some other people's lives as told
by an old bench that has been standing
here and which if it were able to talk
would certainly have a great deal to
relate regarding the entire community's
life for some three or four generations The old
bench stands here in all kinds of weather As if
grown by nature A witness to strange
happenings throughout the year Here
fingers were twined Here old yarns were
worn threadbare Here people howled
at the moon and here people joined hands
And the old writer knew all these things
Oh! if only he could write! But you must judge
now I think this subject has missed being
treated again and again In this way—
at any rate Remember my name is hyphen-
ated Hope you won't dump the whole thing
back in my lap But that's what you'll un-
doubtedly do since I don't have connec-
tions with publishers or anyone else In
advance I thank you

                                        N.C.

In a White Kayak

Thought I was alone
walking by myself
along the canal
Someone came up beside me -
and we decided to
join each other.

I wanted to take
his arm
Thought we were going to
join each other
His arm disappeared
He disappeared
Sat by himself
White in a white kayak
in a tight little manhole ᴗ
Definitely just room for one.

Thought I was alone
He stood beside me:
"Can't a man
have a minute to himself
in his small kayak
without you imagining
all sorts of things?"

Could not know
it was only a minute
Afterward it was too late
to start believing—
Now I can hardly believe
I am alone

Yes, to join
a man like that

takes the faith
of a mustard field
or ability to walk
on water—

My dreams should have
taught me that

But I keep on walking
along the canal
looking for kayaks.

N.C.

Ivan Malinovski

(1926)

I VAN MALINOVSKI has studied languages and literature and has translated among others Pasternak, Chekhov, Nezval, Brecht, Enzensberger, Södergran, and Pablo Neruda; his most important translations of poetry have been collected in the anthology *Glemmebogen* (The Book About the Forgotten). As a poet he is an internationalist and a socialist, influenced by Swedish and Finnish modernism as well as of the short forms of the Far East.

Important collections of poems: *Galgenfrist* (Short Respite) 1958, *Poetomatic* (Poetomatic) 1965, *Leve som var der en fremtid og et håb* (Living As If There Were a Future and a Hope) 1968, *Kritik af tavsheden* (Critique of Silence) 1974.

Love Poem

"Att ständigt vara de sista på jorden ständigt de första"

I
Not only the world
my love
not only the light I drink with others
the railings, the steps we wear away
not only the air they breathe
and their meaningless history
in which I too have my roots

not only these walls
the fears that come nearer
because they are far away

155

not only the world
my love
but also you

you who are different
from all that's occurred and will occur
distant at my side
you the sick man's longing:
the tree behind the windowpane

if I forget you
it is because I remember you too well
may I never remember you
as I remember the world

II
Not only you
my love
but also the world

not only the clock's loud cry from the corner
and the terrible picture
of a white face under your skin

and the white faces behind your shoulder
and the haunted shadows in your eyes
and complaints you yourself know nothing of

clouds you have not seen
days we have not shared
always something else
never we ourselves

our hands are ashamed
as if a stranger stood in the room
suddenly someone weeps in Aramaic
suddenly the sky is a wide-mouthed roar

I know it: somewhere
this house is already tallied
as two numbers on a casualty list

and with good reason distracted
I come to you

                                        N.C.

The Petrol Heart

Ahead (naturally) death
In the rear mirror landscape on landscape
Consumed fields and towns
Stood-up girls
Waste products
Spent time
Blue smoke
Gas
Destination a world of excrement
Enormous kitchen middens
Don't ask why
You burn parents
Gorge yourself with teachers and idols
Gramophone records
Designed paperbacks
You have also got an intellectual arsehole
Whether the brakes work
Is of lesser importance
But constipation is a mortal sin
Your life a meal of petrol
Hastily consumed
Self-service
Accelerator on the floor
A load of seventy years
Must pass through your pupils

You must drink a lake
Digest seven oxen
Thirty acres of forest
In the form of newspapers
Chew your way through a hole botany
Platinum or plastic:
Get it down
The balance of nature
Depends on that
And the future of the Free World
Don't ask why
Ahead
Even greater fields and markets
Landscape on landscape
Perfectly ordinary
Landscapes
Of unknown duration
The scissors concealed
Level crossing or the like

In the rear mirror (naturally) nothing but junk
Just admit it:
You inhale life
You are and will remain the eye of a needle
And the thread has two ends

C.K.

Demonstration

They come and say "The demonstration is over"
Can that really be right?
They come and say "Back to work"
You have heard something quite different
They come and say "Move along"
But should you?
It often happens that they make a mistake
They too are human
Sometimes they do not understand at all
There have been cases where they obviously protected the
    wrong people
It is obviously their duty to be a little slow and a little short-
    sighted
What would happen if a truncheon began to think?
You think for them
In a way you defend their humanity by remaining
In reality it is they who defy your orders
Who is in the right is decided not by philosophy, too late by
    history and never by the radio news
It is decided in the street
It is a matter between you and them
At what point high politics fallout and heavy industry begin to
    carry more weight than police regulations is your
    decision
Alone
They are not in a position to choose
Where they stand stands Rome
Their strength begins at an arbitrary point in a house with
    telephones
Where yours begins hope begins

C.K.

Critique of the Way of the World

Churches disappear between skyscrapers
Castle spires are seen no longer
Among industry's chimneys. Rulers
Replace rulers. When
Will the rulers be replaced?

C.K.

Critique of Distraction

U.S.A.'s crimes against, for example, Indochina
Are known to most. But when I read tomorrow
That 100 persons are feared drowned
By a flood in Missouri, I am pleased
Before I manage to think. This brutalization
That cries to heaven is U.S.A.'s
Crime against me.

C.K.

Critique of Myself

As I returned to Spain, drunk
I did not go out but to bed
At the bad hotel. After midnight
I awoke, turned on the tap and
To my disappointment water came out of it.
"Franco still functions" I said
To myself "And so must you"

C.K.

Critique of the Child Slayers

A small motor which should run
For many years without ever cutting out
Starts ten weeks after conception
What great enemies are not standing ready
With sleeves rolled up:
Schools armies churches hunger factories
States coldness darkness banks and newspapers
What odds on the world champion!
That human beings are still alive
On earth today
Is a fact that fills me
With joyful wonder and' secret thoughts
For the future

            C.K.

Critique of Freedom

The hop twines to the left, as does
The honeysuckle, irrespective of the rulers'
Discretion and the currency situation
Out of a child you can make an adult
Out of woman a delicatessen
Out of a human being in general anything at all
Even a human being

            C.K.

Critique of Reason

All over the world there are small rooms
Where people mate, stubbornly
In spite of all reason

            C.K.

Critique of Long-suffering

The dromedary bites the unjust
Rider. The brooding tree is a sphere
From which even the little fly catcher
With the courage of a wild beast drives away
Much larger birds. We
Allow our dwellings to be defiled, for example
By Nixon's picture on the screen, day
After day, year after year. Too long
Is man's long-suffering

C.K.

Critique of Silence

fallow, tongue-tied, hostile land!
enzensberger

The traitor is taciturn
The receiver, the opportunist.
He who does not join the small birds'
Outcry against the owl
Sides with the owl
"It is my duty to speak
I will not be an accomplice"
Said Zola. Even the pig
Speaks its mind
When it is slaughtered. In Denmark
Reigns a traitorous
Silence, too great for a country
Of its size

C.K.

Critique of Defeatism

In my time triumphed the old
What a line of monarchs—from Hitler to Nixon!
In my time Auschwitz was erected
And Hiroshima dismantled. Space
Became populated and cities were made uninhabitable
And extortion and excretion assumed
Hitherto unknown dimensions.
                                    But also in my time
The mute swan became gregarious and China
Was taken over by the Chinese. As yet
Anything can happen.

                                                    C.K.

Ove Abildgaard
(1916)

OVE ABILDGAARD was influenced by his childhood expe-
riences in a bay-side town in North Jutland. He works
for the Danish radio and has among various translations also
published a Danish version of Goethe's *Faust* (1968).

His chief collections of poems are *Uglegylp* (Pellet) 1946,
Sommerens ekko (The Echo of Summer) 1954, and *Og Lises
hånd i min* (And Lise's Hand in Mine) 1972.

Terndive

A midsummer morning
in Zealand

Nightingale
Whitethroat
Thrush
an underwood of chirping sparrows
in the middle of a choir of joy
I wake.

Then I remember
the morning of childhood.

Doves cooing
Jackdaw chatter
Gulls crying
and deep echoing chug of motors
from cutters on their way
out to sea.

And like a tern
I dive far down
into the depths of memory
bob up with childhood in my beak:

Green shards of bottles in the wilderness
                    of the raspberry bush,
a white rabbit
with eyes like the night light on the kitchen stairs.
The warmth of the horses in the stall,
and anxiety of running the gauntlet of their hooves.
Admiration for the blacksmith who puts them in his lap.

The smell of tobacco and licorice for Lemvig-snuff
mixed with the scent of the baker's newbaked bread,
the coach-builder's dry sawdust,
and the wool-spinner's greasy threads in the filter of the loom.
And through everything the taste of salt from the sea.

Lukewarm seaweed forests about the legs,
shoals of dense-swarming shrimp, and sticklebacks' sting,
the tar bubbling on the planks of the wharf
and red crabs sidelong up against the posts—
a flounder's head on a line, and they grab and clutch.

The sea's caresses and' exhalation in your face ⁃
the desert sand of the dunes through the hourglass of your hands
the jabbing knives of the lyme grass,
the sun turns time back to flotsam
dashed up between grinding pebbles.

A stranded ship, a stranded mine
amber from ancient woods for a tawny neck.
And there Venus rises from the foam
midway between two breakers, whose granite
sea tongues lick like horses blocks of salt.

Venus . . . . .

Venus, who later . . . . .

The tern, satisfied, settles down to rest
on the corner of a well-box.

The songbirds grow silent
only the sparrows still twitter
a pair of ducks pass over the house
like a knife through linen . . .

                                                                        A.T.

Winter Dream

Kale growing in snow
sun veiled in mist
a single hare.

Cordwood
chimneysmoke
a woodpecker in a tree . . .

Tobogganning children
dogs baying
a single hunter.

Lise's hand in mine.
                                        A.T.

12 Eggs

There the rat by the nest
in the henhouse, naked legs,
timid eyes, twelve eggs.
And under ground the young.

The hens cackle, nod,
cackle, nod in unison:
"Law and order," "Law and order."
The cock crowing on high.

A.T.

Jørgen

The half-light between the pine trees,
on a branch near the trunk
a horned owl with feathers on his brow,
owl-droppings spread
over the soft resilient needle-floor
under the resin dripping
spruce trees.
Admiral and brimstone butterflies
in the heat-shimmer over the heath,
adders making their way through the heather.
We with ether bottle and net,
a zero point of being—and Being—
until the clock tears us loose.
There you are, Jørgen,
in the ditch with your bicycle,
its back wheel humming between the blades of grass.

A.T.

Thorkild Bjørnvig
(1918)

THORKILD BJØRNVIG has written monographs on Rilke (1946) and Martin A. Hansen (1964). He is a doctor of philology. He has translated Rilke and Hölderlin and published several collections of essays on literary and artistic subjects. In 1974 he wrote a novel *Pagten* (The Pact) about his friendship with Karen Blixen (Isak Dinesen).

Collections of poems: *Stjærnen bag gavlen* (The Star Behind the Gable) 1947, *Anubis* (Anubis) 1955, *Figur og ild* (Figure and Fire) 1959, *Vibrationer* (Vibrations) 1966, and *Ravnen* (The Raven) 1968). In 1975 a new collection of poems *Delfinen* (The Dolphin) was published.

The Ballad of the "Great Eastern"

I
Not a clipper ship "Ariel," no, an iron hull, issued
from the engineer's point of sight, power perspective, a Yahweh
originated his leviathan, and wrote to the captain:
"Not a ship—a machine shall ply the ocean!"

Brunel: suspended with his wife in a chair above an abyss
to encourage despondent men building one of the daring bridge
      spans—
a lover of Vergil, nature and his green estate in the country—
cut through the fertile farmlands with ribbons of rails

till the belching trains crossed Vergil's pastorals:
The conqueror's private life—or a schizophrenic case?
Erected hospitals in the Crimea, invented weapons:
Charity, patriotism—or indifferent genius?

168

Conceived in his restless ambitious brain: The "Great Eastern,"
a ship larger than any—a maniacal structural vision
possessed him, all things were riveted into its hull of iron:
Vitality, fortune, estate—Brunel, broken beyond recognition,

paralyzed taken ashore on its day of departure—
This vessel of the amphibious century: Sidewheels,
propellers, and bellying lofty sails between smokestacks
like cherubim among furnaces, sparkling and fiery.

II

Down in the holds and topside on deck the crew struggled with
unwieldy iron bars, blocks and tackles, chains and hatches,
with theory—officers practiced with the convenient steering
charts and instruments: vigilant guides and watches.

The victims of theory waved from the wharf: the survivors
of the crew at a windlass ready to haul the ship
for the sideways launch—who, struck by the runaway handle,
lay killed at one stroke or in hospital, bloodsoaked and mangled.

The trumpet signal "The Roast Beef of Old England" summoned
to luncheon in the enormous saloon: a sumptuous
ceremonial hall, pierced by a stack sheathed in mirrors,
arabesques and panels, which concealed its form and function.

Not indicative screening; rather a camouflage for
the volcanic element—teak and absorbing fabrics, marble
to screen off the awareness of gaping fire doors, pinions,
gigantic brutal thighs of the pitmans, the engines' demand for
        oblations.

A valve for the cylinder jacket accidentally closed—and suddenly:
Whirling splinters and steam in the—by chance deserted—saloon
But five stokers burned to a crisp in the forward boiler room
brief screams in the deep black cauldron, where they just
        happened to be.

III

The captain played the flute, or grand piano of rosewood
for his passengers,—but on mild or pleasant nights
a shrill cornetist and chorus of sailors blared through the open
      skylights
from the deck of the "Great Eastern," at last on its ocean crossing:

A floating palace with a view of the squares of the ocean
and sunsets; to dine behind a pane of glass, the display
of the elements viewed in a frame of safety,
to promenade and change dress for an evening party.

On the platform above the sidewheel the passengers stood
      enchanted,
as though from outside the ship, they saw it plying ahead,
spectators even at that—demigods, Goliards, poets,
because to them the inertia felt like their own omnipotence,
      gliding.

Then raised New York: Salutes and sirens, flotilla of boats.
in port the vessel crumpled the piers like paper.
Sightseeing Americans satisfied hungry remembrance,
cut out arabesques and paintings—for souvenirs.

Manslaughter, fighting, and falls through hatches, drunken cruises,
lawsuits and flooded stores—Vine Hall, with sensitive hand
for keys on piano and flute: Engineer, astronomer, captain,
fell ill, and it all slipped reeling from his command.

IV

But the newspapers valued the ship: a gold mine—denied it a
      chance
before it was launched, but praised it highly when floated,
announced its arrival when long overdue, debunked and ex-
      tolled it,
declared it sunk, when in no distress at all.

The third time out came the storm. The giant, planned to be
      larger
than waves, unshakable as a firmament or an island of rocks,
equipped like a home and filled like a warehouse with unlashed
      cargo
was set pitching and yawing and rolling with blows and shocks—

The sidewheels were bent or torn off, the rudder chain burst
      asunder
the sternpost ruptured, the lifeboats washed from the deck,
the jury sail rent,—a swan escaped, blew into the saloon,
flew dazzlingly up and fell down at the wall with a broken neck.

The grand piano rolled hither and thither and crashed with
      a crazy
cacophonous rattle—the vessel, awkward and monstrous, trembled
and grew to the touch, like a nightmare, could only obey
the laws of the current, the storm and the mountains of water
      and spray.

Blue rockets and flares: Then a brig sailed up within earshot—
Rich men, who believed in the power of gold over ego,
reason, and hurricane, screamed from the railing:
"If you take us aboard, I will purchase your ship and your cargo."

V
Sometimes men's dreams of greatness beget a changeling,
breeding in turn a host of grimaces of grandeur, chimeras:
luxury ark, sale to Napoleon III, haremship, warship,
chased by constructors, captains, and shareholders.

The greatest: mere framework: the empty and aimless
became epidemic—the lawless spread like infection:
transport of troops, mutiny, show, and circus raged
through rigging and holds, saloon and the rows of cabins.

And everyone, almost, was prostituted performing the task, just
to render himself of service—stupefied, criminal, overwrought
by filling the frame, by moving the frame—the best and the
          worst have
unseeingly fancied and wished, designed and thought,

while opulence flowed into Europe in torrents, Baudelaire
hurled himself against the black figurehead of his dreams,
the Opium War broke out, children toiled in the clammy caverns
and in Wales and the Ruhr the coal welled up in streams.

The Great Eastern completed one task: the Atlantic Cable, at
          once increasing
the pace of life, political tensions, price fluctuations, affluence,
          debt.
And then it was scrapped: Nietzsche's year in Turin. In West-
          minster Abbey
huge, pharaonic, glowed a stained glass window, a prince's
          honor: Brunel.

Epilogue to the Great Eastern

It went for scrap, for recasting—the remnants:
Ship's bells, teapots, lamps,
the binnacle: temple complete with British
lion of brass,
placing his paw on a globe—
the genii of science on allegorical panels,
the captain's stateroom,
a paddlewheel here and a paddlewheel there,
distributed over taverns, gardens, and country estates:
Greateasterniana!
Long ago the ruptured stack was sunk in a dam
at a waterwork, serving as strainer:
Like pieces of columns from collapsed temples
built into the stone quays of Caesarea.

"Great Eastern,"
once praised by Whitman and Longfellow,
subject of Melville's and Jules Verne's
skeptical diary notes—
slowly repressed,
traumatic: ad acta,
a European family scandal—
and in the family album
the picture of the black sheep, with sparse
lexical comments,
perhaps an empty rectangle:
repression and shame ⚊
among serious bourgeois deities,
but viewed from another level
an allegorical feast at court
for humoristic demons,
forgotten only for other feasts—

Curio, whirled up
into the stream of consciousness by illustrated magazines—
copy, like Leonardo's useless inventions,
Goethe's women.

Strictly speaking christened Leviathan
like Job's and Melville's monster,
larger than Noah's ark (its tonnage computed by Newton),
prelude to ships, named
Polyphemus, Medea,
Marat and Titanic,
names like hammers—
fool's ship, ship of death:
Found at last between heavy plates
the skeletons of a riveter, missing for a generation,
and of an apprentice, forgotten.
It is necessary to rivet—

navigare necesse est—
non vivere.

I.S.

Dysphorial Obituary
Griswold on Poe 1849:

Now he is dead, and simply by surviving
I prevail. Now it is I alone
who shall determine all, his fame, and more
important, reputation, I interpret
his life, decide what happened. Well, now he shall
be recompensed for all his arrogance,
disdainful cleverness and sophistry,
his feverish vehemence when contradicted,
the envy burning on his cheeks when others
were lucky, his dishonorable conduct,
ability to make the rest believe
he was a genius, seraphic demon
and diabolic seraph—well, no matter.
Now I will tear up, shake out his past,
the crystal palace with the stuffy cellars,
with white star lapidation I will blind it
and dump its motivations into the street,
a pile that stinks and testifies to what
he was, in fact, and who he was:
a cynic, radiating frigidity—
the ambition of the friendless, a seducer
and sadist, masochist, sponger and swindler
to blame for his ailing child-wife's death:
genteelish shabby home, consumptive coughing
while he in dread of care escaped in drink,
neglect and a night's repentance at the grave—
(*she* was an angel); drunkard and drug addict—
he has deserved it, yes—out with the truth

he hid behind a frosty, noble pose,
mystification, tragic and sublime—
now I will tear to shreds the silken curtain
with sickly arabesques which softly waving
conceals perfumed and alien chambers filled
with half-spoiled love, 'orgasms of the soul   ⌐
next to a marble-like and ice-cold corpse,
the metamorphoses of hybrid unnature shall
be aired. I will obliterate, deny
him, all that he believed, his prideful heart,
unbounded tenderness, deceits and lies,
my contradiction will clean up the cosmos
with whirling knife agleam, scrape hell and heaven
clean of all trace of him, who thought the center
of the pulsing universe was *our own heart*:
such earnestness blasphemous, absurdly funny—
will smash to bits the instrument
which he called Israfel's: it's nothing other
than imitation, all the works he wrote
I will annihilate and make unwritten,
oblivion enveloping this monster,
layer on layer like Lethean ash
monotonously drizzling down about him
until I get that thorn pulled from my eye,
out of my flesh and end the pain: he who thought
I was his friend, while he displaced *me*, I
the man, who always held the right opinion
wrote on soundness—what the times required—
and soulful piety, edification.

He *was* my friend, his eyes, so large and handsome,
his nobleness, enchantment of his words
when he forgot himself, and I
was carried right along—I pull out the thorn—
his inadmissible trust: I
as executor, after all the scenes,

my grudge and his unseeing arrogance
I publishing his works, perverse, insane,
conceited foolishness: I pull out the thorn.
As if by *trusting* he could paralyze me!
I see right through him, what I say is true,
it is mere justice, and I can breathe again—
and Edgar Allan Poe is dust to dust.

                                                    I.S.

Frank Jæger
(1926)

FRANK JÆGER was educated as a librarian. He translated classics like Molière, Corneille, and Goethe. He has written a great number of plays for radio and television and several short stories of playful imagination with motifs from a vanished Danish idyll.

His chief poetic works are *Dydige digte* (Virtuous Poems) 1948, *Morgenens trompet* (The Trumpet of Morning) 1949, *Tyren* (Taurus) 1953, *Havkarlens sange* (The Merman's Songs) 1956, *Cinna* (Cinna) 1959, and *Idylia* (Idylia) 1967.

Sunday in September

The owl swoops down upon its prey.
Kissing it first from far away
with its tongue:
Then slicing with the bill
and gripping in the claw.
Smells the blood
and sees it.

The owl sits in the tree, crying.
The owl's full, and it's sitting and crying.
Autumn. Autumn.

P.B.

To a Sensitive Girl Friend

Going through the dark to say a
warm and strong hello to these your
hands.
In the deep interiors of my
mind are all good things like burning
brands.

Evil words were pumped out of my
veins in all too many long, long
years.
Words I used at that time when my
heart was sweetened by your maiden
tears.

All good words and all the silence
which is beautiful I kept by
choice.
And a violent longing for the
good words and 'the silence in your
voice.

In the deep interiors of my
mind Joy, a child with white teeth,
stands.
Running through the dark to say a
warm and strong hello to these your
hands.

                                        P.B.

The Afternoon of the Faun in the Park

Madam, your unchaste hand makes me sad
and makes me ache to go away.

Should you not walk in an aged garden
picking red currants or the dim black ones?

With a chip basket on the gravel path, black straw hat
against your white hair and a veil round your chin.

But aren't you happy with husband and home,
do you not love your lovely children any longer?

Your dear big boy whom I cheat
every single day at dice and cards.

Your two sweet daughters, whom every night
I've humiliated far more than I meant to.

Madam, your unchaste hand makes me sad.
You wanted to be like a mother to me...

P.B.

Small Sun

Small sun these weeks.
February has made us smaller.
Snow that weighs. Ice that crushes.
We can prevent nothing.

We cannot pray, either,
to be made bigger.
Starling and mouse and winterwheat
must ask in our place.

But maybe April will fetch
back our hearts' fires.
Together we'll wait patiently for
small sun these days.

                                        P.B.

But in September

Blindly I rushed around in virgin gardens.
a goat in a nursery.
The flowerbed colors were slipping
and August disappeared.

But in September a summer's
overload left
the limbs of the lovely girls,
and the lamps were put on.

Now maybe a fine and frozen
bitterness lives on their lips
and is a sloe to be picked,
and apples all the rest.

Girls, waiting
in the lamplight on gravel roads.
Stronger than all flowers is
the fragrance of my longing toward you.

Through which windows
shall I see dawn again
and harsh morning?

P.B.

Lover

We live in the flesh and want flesh
and we shouldn't forget it.
I sought you here, behind
the black dense hawthorn hedge.
I weighed you
and found your supple lightness. ⁃
A lovely contrast
to the burden of these bushes.

Over me hovers your face,
and the wings of your hair
mingle in my eyes
with the twigs of the hedge.
Still farther off I see
the skies bursting.
Unborn stars are born
for me, your conqueror.

You—straight as a straw
strutting in the spring wind.
You—generous as the tree
abounding in fruit.
You—pallid under your hair,

and with your soul's ravines
laid open to my heart,
the tired traveler.

Blessed for the seeker
is surrender.
Bliss for the tired man
dizzily to beg
wings of a winged being,
and to find his heaven here
where this world is pressed
against his body.

The cockcrows of the farms
lift scarlet and shining.
On the road the horse of dawn
with rags round its hooves.

                                        P.B.

Sidenius in Esbjerg

I am here to become
acquainted with the storm.

The storm radiating
over the Jutland realm.

I am here because
it must happen in Esbjerg's harbor:

a word from the troubled sea
must overwhelm.

Questions hanging
in scared boats' rigging.

In engines the word groans,
in brass it rings:

Who can distinguish here
between judgment and bliss?

Is Death heavier chains?
Is Death wings?

                                    P.B.

Children Sing like This

We did not want to be,
and yet we are.
Stones knock together
and sparks leap out.

Stalk of fruit, September
nightsound falls in grass.
Thread of star, October
late rain of light rains.

We did not want to be,
we are just the same.
Also what's most bitter:
we're a threat, a worry.

The peaceful hare,
and there: its flight.
In front of us grows
in our shadow its fear.

We saw behind it all,
we owned an eternity.
What do we see now,
a day, nothing.

Go back, oh if we might.—
This the heart's strong longing.
We did not want to be,
and yet we're here.

                              P.B.

Jørgen Gustava Brandt
(1929)

JØRGEN GUSTAVA BRANDT was born in the heart of
Copenhagen; he is a painter, flaneur, and dandy. He works
at Denmark's radio and has translated among others Henry
Miller and Dylan Thomas.

He has published more than ten volumes of poems, collections
of essays, short stories, and the two novels *Kvinden på Lüneburg
Hede* (The Woman on the Lüneburger Moors) 1959, and *Pink
Champagne* (Pink Champagne) 1973.

Sound of Bell

They put out her lamp, which kept out the city
from their meeting. In an alluring wall a bell struck
                                                    firmly
against the evening mists in the Botanical Gardens (over there)
and the skydark grew tight up to the two who were
                                                    together.

The bodies of their souls, the souls of their bodies
                                        met,
that is to say: they screwed like angels
and they exchanged their secrets with lips, tongues,
                                        visages, and sexes.

Then came the hush. Shapes approached. In the
                                        window
the extinguished houses, three trees, with the faceless gray,
awaiting . . . But far out there a street glided
                            away, shiny, empty,

cold, sliding into distance and miles...

He has forgotten her face. She has forgotten his face.
He has forgotten her name. She has forgotten his name.

A.T.

Come Aboard

Your bluedazzling glance
from the boat
the lakeshore's glittering leaves
behind your face, shining
with natural joy

In the high woods noisy naked children run
horizontally they flicker past
through the verticals

The world opens to me
as I come aboard to you
and yet everything is as it is

I see my shadow darting under me
in the water
and under my shadow another
—gliding under us
as I step into the boat

The moment flashes white
We are only smiles
in each other's smiles:
face to face
in the boat

—My love.

A.T.

My Element

To sit on the terrace on course on this spot with calm pulse. Without taking notice of them I see well enough the other sailing light worms in the summer night which/nearly unnoticeably closes in/ Some dart off so that you merely catch a glimpse of twinkling through the leaves, others stand almost still in the twilight. From the open window of the house I now hear Dexter Gordon's splendid round hornsound come flowing. Almost motionless I dance without the people nearby knowing the least thing about it. A huge warm silent, breathing cunt has spread out over me. Here I am truly in my element, I exist as a blind softly pushing, floating possibility and fulfill my purpose to perfection, a full, resolute radaring, sniffing quiver here
in this closed world.

A. T.

Night Hour of Suchness

Night hour of suchness
your plans are forgotten
you hardly live in anybody's dream
and the day lies distant, in the past.

Night hour of delight
even book, music, cigar are forgotten
you came past your name, the names
the familiarity of notes, the cessation of sounds
the smoke's movement, the ash—
now you are on the other side of stillness.

Night hour well on into the small
hours. The last talk incomprehensible
distant distraction, lies back there
in historical impenetrability
like the first Christian centuries of the North.

Night hour where everything near is asleep
only spaces of spaces seem awake.

Night hour of soul's anesthesia
the smallest things peeled down to suchness
the whatness of the details of objects
the pattern of the caning on the essential
marvelous chair, charred matchstick's charredness
but also large flower-on-the-windowsill's
flowerlargeness
and out there, under the streetlight-streetlight
the shadows more shadowlike
and the house next door more closed dark and houselike

Night hour where the least creaking
of the beards, the wood of the furniture
would be the deepest violation
of everything that is important
an inadmissible cry of dissonance
—or perhaps just
the wood's sigh, the timber's complaint
of homesickness for the forest

Night hour when all doors are locked
and awareness open like a worktool's workshop

Night hour of grace
where nakedness is the only possible clothing.

Night hour where the remembered words
about truth, about beauty
are diffused in the air
where your veins are the channels of silence
where you breathe in suchness like a scent
where all your efforts like the distant day
is the tape recorder's clean sound
frenetic scarcely audible whirring
and where the direction of your prayer doesn't matter.

A.T.

You

Saw in you
one seeking wanting to be found   ⌐

come!

A.T.

The House in Copenhagen

The staring of fever, where ghosts are soberly
reflected before the mirrors explode;
city of my awakening, which sank
in fanfare, sirens and oblivion . . .

I accept *me*, and childhood,
my room at night, alone
with me and the clock, which struck
twelve, one . . . three . . .
. . . and seen, from the depth of generations
silent, through the window:
the snowdecked roof of the dark . . .
—Or sudden insight:
the stairwing's smell of summer and provisions,
when you seldom came there
from the country
And the tree out back, luxuriant and green
Midsummer Eve.

Then try me again, house, tree, lineage, universe,
my love is penance, joy, fearless.
Time to sleep, time to drink,
time to work. Abundance. Certainty.

Whatever everything is, it is devotion.
If not in us, there is no altar;
I have unburdened myself of it.

Look, our daily lives were like a sacrifice of lamb,
bulls, oil, coins, this substitution,
(what the ancients used) and view and sight.
Sacrificing now—where we know
                    the accomplished, concluded
forms,—substitution is impossible.
                    You stand in the day.
Give day your light.

                              J.G.B./A.T.

Patience

A method of waiting
without awaiting anything
to keep a fire alive
under a streaming heaven.

                              A.T.

Out of Nothing You Come Walking

Out of nothing you come walking
as in a dream
out of nothing you come
softly walking

out of the dark you step
like a shadow of light

not of the sun, not
of the lamps' night
but out of nothing, softly walking
A.T.

Evident

—Let me touch you
You have been very lonesome very long,
therefore I trust you now

In the world of man
the wrong ones possess the power
And it is the wrong ones
who want it
—Power is necessary
—That problem is yours

—I don't want *you* to be different
—Then we must take counsel!

—Let the world be like you
—You are the life and the truth
J.G.B./A.T.

It Is the Bird in the Tree

It is the bird in the tree that is most important
It is the tree with the bird that is the most important
It is the tree and the bird that are the most important
That I see the tree and the bird in the tree

That the tree and the bird are there when I see them
That I know you see the bird in the tree and the tree
That it is us who see the tree with the bird
That's it, it is the bird in the tree that is important

That we become us who see it while we are seeing it
It is the bird in the tree that is the most important
It isn't us, it is the bird in the tree
It is the tree with the bird that is the most important

It is the tree and the bird that are so right
It is the music in this ordinariness that is
It is this bird and this tree that are so important
It is the music in the ordinariness that is mystical

It is the mystical ordinariness that is the music
It is the ordinariness in the music that is the right thing
It is its being there which is so important
It is that which isn't there which is so important

It is the ordinariness which is so mystical
There is no bird and no tree that is important
That I see the tree and the bird are not important
That we become us who see it is not the most important

It is the ordinariness behind the sign that is present
It is the errors in the account that are so inimitable
It is the ordinariness of the sentence that is nutritious
The incomparable is the trivially present

Here by the window there are no whole of half circles
By the window there is the tree with the bird, which is the
       most important
There are no equal lines in the pickets of the fence
There is nothing straight about the wires of the poles
                      (which-also-sing)

A tree is a tree—
This ordinary tree is different than others
All ordinary trees are different
This tree with this bird is here (also in me)

                                     A.T.

Per Højholt
(1928)

PER HØJHOLT was born on the west coast of Jutland; he is a librarian and art critic. He tours with an audio-visual poetic "show" based on language, electronics, and beat effects.

Among his works are the critical essay *Cezannes metode* (Cezanne's Method) 1967, and the collections of poems *Hesten og solen* (Horse and Sun) 1949, *Poetens hoved* (The Head of the Poet) 1963, *Min hånd 66* (My Hand 66) 1966, *Turbo* (Turbo) 1968, and the concretist collage *Volumen* (Volume) 1974.

November

Not that snow is falling and it is rather cold weather
blowing, troubles me, oh my blackbird.
Nor even that the pond
under the cherry trees near the track
fades and drifts over. November is like that.
But that this morning you sat cold in the magnolia
like a heart encircled by ribs
suddenly in snowbanks or decay.

N.C.

M/S Nelly in Countersound

White over my emotions' abstract landship
suicideseal. Glimmering like liquor in water
my hand against these "hard facts":

194

The cupboard stinks of my emotions' deeds
and everyday trivialities: Teak. Tick.
Mathema. Themathema. Mathtac. Thematic.

Anatematack. Anagrick. Atomatack. Ick
everydays' inexhorable *avancement*
house and home overfelt and underloved.

My hand in water like liqueur shimmering
A "fact": Suicidesun white
over my emotions' abstrick lindship.

Nelly. Nelly. Nelly. NELLY.

                                        N.C./A.T.

Outside

stand backward at the top & begin from the bottom
back and can't be there & must ultimately yield &
one after another gradually till we ourselves draw
but they're difficult to get in place must be set
about to be finished we lack but the final twelve
but absolutely safe & completely leak-proof we are
I believe that above they're thin extremely frail
in relation to those on the other side too oh yes
thickness but still tighter that is to say firmer
those on top of them that are quite comparable in
much especially pressed down now by the weight of
away they fill up a little more room & weigh damn
build a foundation beneath those we start to take
in can we place the farthest down in position and
only when we are assured that nothing is pressing
we begin at the bottom & then work our way up but
                                        N.C.

So and so Many Larks

383 larks have come 384
tops of birch trees seethe (385) like balloons actually balloons
    which you blow up gas deposits on stems curtsying like
    birchtrees yes exactly like birchtrees that seethe
388 larks have come and sing over molehills 389
the routes that winter takes in its sleep are exposed lie exposed
    and full of water the sun strikes them
a morris drives up over the hill and down and rumbles through
    the sunken road and approaches splashing along the
    pine trees
the mailman's morris comes into view under 390 larks

                             N.C./A.T.

A 5-pinnate Leaf

pavement the stones absolutely fresh on the inside newly-spilt
    sun absolutely fresh over morning-wet rye
knife-jingling swallows in the gate irritable needles of the
    swallows under the chestnuts
tiled roofs are blended into sea/wood's edge/tiled roofs yonder
    a glimpse of the enormous whale of the trivial landscape
    a hill's shadow
In the afternoon you see nothing at all you steal along the
    horizon as a knife you lie on the stones down at the
    beach and talk to your wife about Pnin
hey John has gone up I think John has gone up to the attic
    John has gone up to the attic to compose a poem oh
    well! indeed!

                             P.B.

The Poet H

skeletonized juniper too morbid fir moss bells
the brook a cloud of bells hanging in the grass

cloud-landing-net for hurrying trawl then a banquet
up there they are enormously drunk and then I Horatio

in the meadow leaned against a caroms table full of zeroes
and at last the poet H – used as a spirit level

P.B.

Frosty Night

while this was written the children in there in their
        beds talked about the stars that mean nothing to us
while this is written later when no one in this house any
        longer talks about stars and their possible meaning
while this that I have written here is about stars and
        their eventual meaning for us humans

P.B.

Turbo 4

henry into the landscape he bows and thanks and goes out again
into the landscape henry he bows and thanks and goes out again
into the landscape he bows henry and thanks and goes out again
into the landscape he bows and henry thanks and goes out again
into the landscape he bows and thanks henry and goes out again
into the landscape he bows and thanks and henry goes out again
into the landscape he bows and thanks and goes out henry again
into the landscape he bows and thanks and goes out again henry
into the landscape again he is given flowers and bows and tips
over and hangs slantwise in the air with the feet upward and
          the cheek
against the hill half half-ripe appendage to the mother-globe half-
way in a recoiling jump from the zero-point henry on edge in
          the role
⮞ of Big Dipper very very visible in trousers and coat up there on
the hill and see now how quietly a cloud tips over and more and
lies down on its back in balance and down there by the brook his
small property with the curtains out the windows and swinging
doors outside and inside his wife rocking with her nails in
          the doorstep
and glares up at him between her tits *henry you shit* henry
with the cheek against the striking surface and flowers in the
          hand smiles
with upside-down dentures and grows and grows and then the
          brook boils up
with crystal-clear cubes and pushes them onto the meadow and
          while
henry (good ole henry tr.n.) grows and grows they pitch into
balance 20 cm. above the grass cube-letters racing off and now
they let loose and edge off from bushes and trees in the grass
          in moss down
beneath them wiggle lit from above brook trout in wet water-
          cress and

delighted henry grins with upside-down eyes and declares *check*
    now now
not a single moment longer they will come all of them and
    they will
park in the trees and there will be fun games and fecundity
till I am entirely clear yes and sure enough dammit his body
    cells and all
does not grow into more henry but a bigger surface w henry-
    points
an enormous anonymous slanted community iridescent like water
    in light
up on the hill and the wife in backwards somersault back to
    the doorstep
the brook trout still and cold in its watercress and punctually
    henry slides
into the landscape again he bows and thanks and goes out henry
into the landscape again he bows and thanks and henry goes out
into the landscape again he bows and thanks henry and goes out
into the landscape again he bows and henry thanks and goes out
into the landscape again he bows henry and thanks and goes out
into the landscape again henry he bows and thanks and goes out
into the landscape henry again he bows and thanks and goes out
henry into the landscape again he bows and tips over and

                                          T.N.

Robert Corydon
(1924)

R OBERT CORYDON is a journalist, painter, and lithographic
artist. He has experimented with the use of calligraphy
in his poetry.

Among his collections of poems are *Hænderne* (The Hands)
1950, *Skrænten mod havet* (The Cliff by the Sea) 1955, *Krybet
og sommerfuglen* (The Creeper and the Butterfly) 1958, *Ord
til havet* (Words to the Sea) 1968, *Kalligrapoetica* (Calligra-
poetica) 1972, and *Jeg var her næsten ikke* (I Was Hardly
Here At All) 1972.

Sea Poem

Always longing fills me
for the ocean's great, pure soul.
The window of the house is an
eternal, watching eye
with a man as
its mirroring pupil.

The sun's white circle
glowing above the ocean's
glazed, green line
and the crushing weight
of water in congealing space.

A black boat that
for days has hewn
its way through the horizon
like a snail on the ridge of day.

200

The sea dilates a mind
in the anguishing wind.
I am an eternally
mirroring pupil
with the sea lurking at my feet.

R.F.B.

Nettles

It was at the bottom
of the white sun's day.
I was a boy
with dusty sandals.

The huge nettles
threatened above me
like a dark green
surf solidified.

A whole day passed
at the nettles' root.
A bird sat
inside the nettle darkness.
An eye burned
itself into mine.

And it was dark
around me when
I heard the call
from the house.

T.N.

Shouts between Two Boats at Sea

They fluttered out over the deeps
like a couple of clumsy birds ...
flitted briefly against the cliff of storm—

And in a moment after we read on the men's faces
that the shouts' uncertain birds
had arrived.

N.C.

Chinese Brush

Black are the shadows sweeping through
the white autumnal night.

The long and short curves
are like calligraphy in space

drawn lavishly by that
wet brush on the stretched white

like the sharp sumi ink
I saw one time

- hotly conjure things to life
on the parchment's pale desert.

Space stands as an invisible vase-shape
with distant cool-blue contours.

The rapid brush of twilight
hurries over autumn's stretched white

as on an old hidden glaze
that sets hard as diamond

in the morning sun's hot oven.

                                                    T.N.

The Sign

There is a slowly
anchoring happiness
in finding a piece of wood
in back of the breakers'
bubbling white basin—

in finding that piece of wood
that snugly fits into your hand,
in carving a mark
and painting with ink
that bushman's sign
which is in your heart.

                                            R.F.B.

Spacecraft R101

A gray whale at its anchor mast
inconceivable man-made in its fastening
in its last earthly kiss to
its authoritarian pylon
‑ its thin silken skin shaking

And this party of cigar-smoking
half courageous half desperate men
in their anachronistic lounges
below the volume of hydrogen

Ready for the eternal prestige race
raised far above that balance which
ought to be here and there . . .
then rather into the Channel's
stormy night and loss of altitude
into a fall on a field in Normandy
so far from its distant Indian goal

The escape stuck to the blueprint
heavy with ambitious outlines for
a wingless whale in the imagination's dry dock
bred for farther transportation in space

sclerotic ambivalence of honor prestige
and macabre ambition

— — —

Astronauts
every time you lift the Earth despite the fall
make space smaller   leap from globe to globe:
it is now reported that your flight succeeded
Moon landing
each time the flight is new and the same

unbelievable man-made
tied to its anchor mast

T.N.

Ocean Riddle

Rain on the ocean
the gray-blue counter of the squall
foams through rows of waves,
out farther, over sand bars,
hurdle after hurdle,
in mist shimmering with sun,
with one gleaming shaft of light
that holds to the rain shower
like a bridle over
the ocean's throbbing mane.

N.C.

Jørgen Sonne
(1925)

JØRGEN SONNE has a university degree in English and History; he has been a grammar school teacher and museum official. He has studied in Europe and in East Asia.

He has translated Arab, African, English, and French literature, among others Ezra Pound, Rimbaud, Lautreamont, and has taken a special interest in Elizabethan literature.

Apart from essays and a single novel he has published seven collections of poems among which are *Delfiner i skoven* (Dolphins in the Wood) 1951, *Krese* (Circles) 1963, and *Thai-noter* (Thai Notes) 1974.

It Is You

It is you, say the eyes.
It is birches, it is sheaves,
say the arms.
It is rainfall, reefs at sea,
say two lips.
It is wing and ash,
says the fingers' trembling.

It is you, says everything.
It is all, says silence.

It is kelp and chanterelle,
resin and wind,
say the wings of the nostrils.
It is chalk and meadow soil,

says the belly's skin. ⌐
It is flying deer,
says the knees' claw.

It is snow, it is surf,
says oblivion . . .

It is the sap-oozing fruit in rage, ◆
says the swelling hidden core.

It is the gate of nations,
says the death-sleep's lightning.

It is thunder in the cosmos,
says the heart of the unborn.

T.N.

The Shepherds' Adoration

He guides the flock in, a faithful shepherd,
while it mumbles applause, in jumbled speech,
and sees itself stand mirrored at the crib.

There, fed with words and hay in bundles,
it endures Florence's arid fires,
trudging and trotting through narrow folds.

But after the flight across flat deserts
this finally is the promised land—
wells out of cooling, boundless springs.

Darkening tree crowns are in their garments
and spring night sky's burning depth;
intense remoteness' opens all around them.   ⌐

Stillness grows, all waiting is at end,
and wonder descends pale as reaped corn;
the heavy shepherds open their hands.

And the angels fly out like white swallows
and sing with joy under the ceiling's scent
of hay and wood and apples, summer consummated.

Bird migrations swing in tips of branches
in trees against a cold sky's white
light over naked fields' edge o' Denmark . . .

We walk away in dreams of your wet winter;
warily you swaddle us in darkness,
and we are near the young cool breasts.

                                                    T.N.

The Fold-out Men

In the plush sofa "The Green Tree"
we looked at grandfather's big medical book—
leaf upon leaf about the fruits of good and evil;
the naked ladies in strange postures,
exciting white bait for children's eyes;
the Snake reared quivering beneath us . . .

We plucked the fruits of eternal death
in the book's jungle, all the possibilities
planted in the Garden here: Rachitis, lepra—
cellar-potato shoots, snowy mouldering pears—
the great harvest's consumption, horror
hissing forth from yellow and black leaves . . .

But a meat-eating botany's herbarium
were the fold-out men: Layer on layer of flaps,

paste-board models of wildest butcheries!
We pulled their skin off, tore their flesh away,
slit open the guts and turned inside-out:
Flamey beds, tidily spread-out sacrifice.

Cannibals of curiosity and wonder;
small lovers, with cut-and-paste fingers—
we saw: Capsules of mirrored organs,
and nets of veins unfolded—blue, red trees—
where our snow-white tree, the hidden skeleton
reposed with smiles in a storybook—

An "Open Sesame!" with pearls and gold,
the Gorgeous Grotto with its moon opal,
the fountain of rubies and sapphires—
it sang and glittered, our eyes plundered
nests and red hearts, hidden in this
Fairytale Christmas tree.

We cracked the shell from the brain's wet walnut;
peeled female skin off the foetal mandarin.
Above barber's-block stare, below belly-eye,
same form and different taste for us:
Mock-turtle meat balls, and a pale head cheese,
against provocative, forbidden, acrid fruit.

(Later we found the brain's command core,
its flawless ticking, its blocking up,
its great lightnings, blasting the wires . . .
Others hung on to the braying goddesses
with the milk bars in front: Bottle babies
rocked on *glamor*, backwards, in Mama's womb.)

An early wake up warning, those studies.
We grew into full-grown fold-out men;
contemplating our navels, *incurvati*,

yearning victims of incisions
we dug out the soul with the knife of torture;
augurs befogged by griefs and glossaries.

Then from the South there landed in our hands
a small young nude woman,' downy-smooth
in yellow polished ivory, oh winter-sun!
An Easter egg, the round belly-lid;
we opened it. And there *you* lay sleeping . . .
You, who have come here, to us both.

Grow, dense seed, in our sun-baked apple!
Rocked, rammed,' Mighty One, break through
in high winds, rising in light, into the soughing
from other trees, harvest-laden with glittering,
floating island in the sky's star foliage!
Our island sank . . . sun-blue the coasts flower forth.
                  T.N.

Birds in the Mountains

I come from nothing,
circling out,
in rising silence
    with sunbeams
from the gorges' sea-green womb—

from dizzying chasms,
swallows' stars,
I lift up clarity—earth olive

and sun liquid on my wing,
sky flame in its quill feathers
    dissolved into light
as shoals of fish descend deep down
where ocean darkens to stone.
            N.C.

Uffe Harder
(1930)

U FFE HARDER is a critic and co-editor of the art magazine *Louisiana Revy*; he works at Denmark's Radio and has published anthologies of French and African poetry and Latin American short stories.

He has translated among others Gustave Flaubert, Tzara, Eluard, Michaux, Beckett, and Claude Simon as well as several Italian and Latin American writers.

From 1945 until 1971 he has published five collections of poems.

Cycling

Cyclists hurtling down deserted roads
fleeting painfully fleeting evasive
things feelings ideas thin as
steel tubes scaffoldings silent whist-
ling wheels spokes stony faces hel-
mets pale faces and wheels soughing and
out of sight but possible faint per-
ceived someplace in the cold dawn words
definitions sensations possible certainty
eternally evasive doubtful certainty the
road like a ribbon before them concrete
and cleaving the air tiny shapes whist-
ling parts of thoughts knowledge a word
feelings sight always one by one one
thing missed because of the next fragment
of impossible impossible always fleeing

wholeness of frail changes rare changing
evasive unclear forms perceived in the
morning mist in the thicket in the fog in
the heatflicker smokescreen the tears the
frenzy the sweat flickering like reflect-
ions chimneys giraffes blown away whisked
away swept away over the fields and the
feet strapped firmly in the pedals the
road behind them like a ribbon

U.H./A.T.

Factors

faces come toward you as though on hand trucks
the factors have a tendency to blend:
a foot comes through the door before the voice
or the voice before the foot
the experience of a person before the person
or the person alone without the experience
the person before the understanding of the person
or the understanding of the person before the person referred to
or somebody quite different.

U.H./A.T.

To Reach out for Pen and Paper

To reach out for pen and paper
to get up take pen and paper
with a look as though saying
is that the telephone again

it is a feeling like going out
when you would rather stay in
like throwing yourself down when you
just climbed up
like beginning a discussion you don't
expect anything from

it is a painful interrogation
a search that you never believed
would lead to anything

To reach out for pen and paper
to straighten up take pen and paper.
                                        U.H./A.T.

Object

A circle
and a larger circle
a handle in the middle but
the sides which slope out
are important too thus
bottom handle sides and the
uppermost brim from which you drink
a yellow brown reddish or greenish
warm almost airy or
colder heavier fluid
on the sides lines are often formed

- fine cracks
the whole of it off white
or some other color
sits on the table or is carried
through the air
If you moved the cup
the tea would hover
or rather sit there
in a truncated cono
with air on almost
every side.

U.H./A.T.

Deep Quiet with Snow

The knocking of waterpipes
deep quiet with snow
falling
past the eye
deep silence
snow like an endless film
to clear the drifts in your mind
quickly covered again.

U.H./A.T.

An Assignment of Icarus

Dedalus, the technician, built a labyrinth for King Minos
    of Crete   .

In several languages the word for elaborate, expert, ingenious
    is derived from his name

and still used.

Later he was incarcerated in the same labyrinth. Imprisoned
with him was his son Icarus, a young man.

Minos, Dedalus said (according to the poet), can seal off land
    and sea.
The sky is always open, that's the way we'll take.
Minos rules over everything, everything except the air.

Then came the work, and Dedalus' advice: too low
and the feathers grow heavy with sea water so you can't lift
        your arm,
too high, and the sun melts the wax so the wings fall apart.
And the flight: Samos, Delos, and Paros,
Lebintos, the honey-rich Kalimnos.

After the first anxiety
he must have been infatuated
by the light, by reflections from the sea and the foam
under him,
the play with the winds and the very possibility
of changing his altitude, the air bathing him,
the easy glide
upward with a turn of the wing,
a labyrinth
of glittering, falling, and rising,
lightness and weight,

the sun burning his back,
the blood buzzing in his ears,
the sweat drying in the wind
the lock of hair that he can't brush away,
the islands that go on changing place,
the white mountains floating on the sea,
a whirl of clouds, of light, of water and sky,
the sound of the beat of his own wings in the air,
the beating of his heart,

far below, Dedalus, in a straight line.

From a distance: a pair of dots, two bodies with wings,
together at first, but then one rises
in an arc, more and more steeply,
until it plunges straight into the sea,
for a while the other flutters over the spot
and flies on, in a straight line, and vanishes.
Too heavy and too big for terns,
and gods would scarcely allow such misfortune to overtake them,
but then who knows?
So something would indicate that they were people.

What happened to the one who didn't drown?

U.H./A.T.

Conditions

Two are fighting. A bigger and a smaller. Two. Each in his own way,
·with his means, his words. For words also play a role in this fight,
although a secondary one. Two have collided and fight. The fight has
rules, but these rules are apparently not the same for the two fight-
ers. Only the fight is the same. The words are not the same, either.
And yet. But, as said, of secondary importance. The first kicks the
second. The second throws sand at the first. That is permissible when
two fight. They try to tear the ears off each other. That's also per-
missible, is respectable when two are fighting. However, the bigger
one has a stick, and this is one of the two points where the rules
seem to differ. The rules for the first and the rules for the second.
As regards the first, the second, and at times the third, for no fight
is fought between just two. The rules, certain of the rules, allow
the bigger one to have a stick, a big stuck, while the smaller one
has no stick, not even a little one. The bigger, who has a big stick,
is not allowed, on the other hand, to use his big stick, or almost
not allowed to, that is, only to a limited extent, now and then. On
the other hand, the big stick is sacred. The smaller one must not
touch it (only it may touch him, although, as said, only now and then,
here and there) not even when it whistles over his head. He may not
knock off the least splinter of it. If he does, the bigger one has the
right to use his stick to a greater extent. So go the rules. Not to
the fullest extent, but to a greater extent. In order to punish the
smaller one who has damaged the stick. Which is sacred. Two are fight-
ing. A bigger and a smaller. One has a stick, one hasn't any. The
stick may not be used, or almost not, may not be damaged, not even
when it is used to a limited extent, now and then, here and there.
It should be held in respect. By the bigger, to whom it belongs, and
by the smaller, on whom it is used, although to a limited extent.
They both must hold the stick in respect. So on that point, when you
think of it, the conditions are the same for the bigger and the small-
er. Perhaps on other points, too. Perhaps, all things considered, it
is only the size that is different.

U.H./A.T.

Cecil Bødker
(1927)

CECIL BØDKER was trained as a silversmith. She has written several novels and collections of short stories as well as the collections of poems *Luseblomster* (Louse Flowers) 1955, *Fygende heste* (Flying Horses) 1956, *Anadyomene* (Anadyomene) 1959, and *I vædderens tegn* (Under the Sign of the Ram) 1968.

She has also written radio plays and children's books which have been awarded prizes and translated into many languages.

Self-portrait

Weeds grow shamelessly
on my tongue
in the middle of a bed
of taste buds,
and between my hair's
mangrove roots
swamp-fish are shoaling
like fugitive silver-green
shadow-animals.

My heart dangles
carefree
on its string
from the lower left rib,
if it gets broken
I'll scatter it
like ashes on the top
of my head—
or maybe
like gunpowder.

A.T.

The Companion

You came to us so quietly from the other bank
and saw us bathe.
Expectantly.
Tempting, you walked on the water
with shining feet.

We knew you—and yet we knew you not.
If you touched us with the shadow
of just one finger
we froze.

For weren't you the one who made the sky ripple,
and was it not your hand
that caught the keel
of the rocking boat of rashness
trying to reach us?

But weren't you also the one
who carelessly
put adventure's taste of iron and earth
in our mouth?
Could you know
we did not know you?

Innocently you sat with us,
farthest out,
on the staggering yellow wood piles
and we did not know who you were.

You kept watching us
you were always the one who was with us
always with him who dared the most,
and we saw you mirrored
in the unsafe ice of the marl pit

and under the fishing rod
on spring days.

We knew you
and yet we knew you not
your being was barbed wire in the grass
and we always walked with bare feet.

                                        T.N.

June Night

Your dusty shadow deserted you
at the threshold of night.
People shut the doors of their houses
and left you alone
with this darkness which was not darkness
which was not light
which was Iceland—in a bygone age,
and where things
your hands touched hours ago
turned into sagas
and together with the whimbrel's wail
told you something
of pale weightless nights
you have never known
and can never forget
and will never meet again.

Only this night
whose sounds were voices you did not understand
whose dew
had fallen a thousand years before your birth
on grass
that never brushed against a shoe
like the one that separated your foot

from a coolness
of an age unfamiliar to you.
Only this one night,
where your unquestioning eyes
faced a land that was lost
which was lived and forgotten
you knew
what had been absorbed like a silence
like an Icelandic awareness
in a consciousness
vaster, more ancient than yours.

N.C.

Under the Sign of the Ram

I,
a landscape with eyesight,
born under the Ram.
Wandering seaweed
from the world sea
unrecognized—

An immense song lies buried
in March,
the echo of an immense laughter
preserved.
But who owns the keys
to the hidden chambers
behind us?

Who dreams there
violent dreams
surrounding my sleep,
and with clay-covered hands
depletes the soil
of my landscape?

Unseen
I must journey on foot
under the sign of the Ram,
come so close to what is smallest
that something will open
opposite.

I,
a landscape with eyesight,
in March.

N.C.

Calendar

One year there were too many
frogs
—and maybe mosquitoes.
People talked about the soil's
increased aquasity
and had it noted
in the calendar.

Last year it was the snails.

And the year before
roving
foxes.

Things will work out, people said:
they'll die off by themselves.
And people talked about mange
and prolonged sickness
starvation
stress
rabies—
it will all come to an end.

Just look at the foxes, people said.

One year there were mice
the next year there were none.
That was proof.

This year it is children.

People talk about the soil's
lack of aquasity
and the blighted grain
people talk about responsibility
and lack of responsibility
people talk—

For things will surely work out
by themselves.
Just look at the foxes
Just look at all the mice—
it goes into the calendar.

Next year it will be flies.

N.C./A.T.

Klaus Rifbjerg
(1931)

K LAUS RIFBJERG has traveled and studied in many parts of the world, for example in the U.S. (Princeton University), and lives periodically in Spain. He is a journalist, film, theater, and literary critic. He has written several plays for television, radio, and theater as well as film scripts.

Several of his novels and short stories have been translated into other languages. Among his chief novels are *Den kroniske uskyld* (Chronic Innocence) 1958, *Operaelskeren* (The Opera Lover) 1966, and *Anna (Jeg) Anna* (Anna [I] Anna) 1969.

He is also the author of the collections of poems *Under vejr med mig selv* (Getting Wind of Myself) 1956, *Konfrontation* (Confrontation) 1960, *Amagerdigte* (Amager Poems) 1965, *Mytologi* (Mythology) 1970, *Scener fra det daglige liv* (Scenes from Daily Life) 1973, and *25 desperate digte* (25 Desperate Poems) 1974.

Birth

Poseur from the start.
With an elegant movement
I unlace myself from the umbilical cord
wound three times around my neck
like a cashmere scarf.

An unpleasant male person
quickly demonstrates this new life's severity
three resounding slaps on the rump.

They try in vain to kill me
under the cold water faucet
but later try a slyer trick—
putting a beer bottle at the foot of my bed.
Despite the tepid water it contains,
desire rises from the green glass
even in these first minutes
through the sensitive balls of my feet. ⌐

Now I am completely independent.
Little bird of passage flown from warmer lands
sitting in his blue nest.

I observe nature on my bedroom ceiling
small shadows of leaves sway
creating faces
friendly portraits upon my first hour's plaster heaven.

Brave new world
I function!
I shit!
soon the gentlest moon is lit
full and opulent over my cradle
the lamp nudges the darkness
and someone lovingly lays bunting
on my damp behind.

Is it perhaps a royal banquet?
Who's been invited?
If only I weren't sleepy.

Like a perfect gentleman
I raise myself on my elbow
tip my imaginary Eden-hat
to my mother:

Thanks, you brooding hen!
Thanks for good partnership,
well rowed!

And sink back drowzily on the pillow,
a strenuous day!

N.C./A.T.

Medieval Morning

Sore throat
and tongue coated by
Middle-Age
childhood pain from
winter coat on the shoulder
and formalin dusting
up from the gravel
with every step.

Dispassionate wandering
under leadership
aware of oneself as heaviness
around painful spots
judo-chop in throat's hollow
spiderweb in larynx
and eyes' acceptance of the
object world, uprooted
mills, fishing cottages, lambs
Middle-Age is rolled off
in gray layers against the
front teeth.

Thus tasted my awakening the
dark in this Bedlam
of relapse, time relapse

pain in the throat
while the alcove was compressed
full of blackness and
I knew that my hands
arms, feet, testicles
perhaps were not there
but tried the voice's
conviction and

told myself that morning's
generality was guaranty enough the
taste   on   the   tongue the
throat's white spots the only light
oh yes, it was true enough
all of it. The

Smell of formalin
from myself, the breath
out over all the small animals
on me, the louse-coziness and
terror of the small sorenesses
that were me.

Now cocks' crow and the fall of iron-curtain,
swing to another perception
candlesticks, tallow
difficulty in seeing through the
panes, but in spite of all
light comes through, the stench
I have become accustomed to, but which
persists, the day's unfelt, muffled
headache and the consciousness of
dirt between two toes this
feeling of guilt. The

Notion about time's classification
Gothic later, lies in the glance
at the cross with Him on it
while a wave runs through the
abdomen below the navel, down over
groin and on the thigh's surface
why so young? The
alcove sticks its tongue out, the
blanket—and crystals of feeling
dissolve, the ritual becomes formal
one is not going to die, the
laughter, oh, its warm hysteria

sits in the cheeks
all sounds are suppressed the
knee joint's little whistle
then the steps, the usual
number and all knowledge about this
ceases, I hear from far away the
hinge-sound, move my shoulder
in one free swing, clear my throat. The sunlight.
I forget me.

T.N.

Zeus in that Mood

About true virtues
one must speak simply, my dear.
Listen:
I love you
for your lovely eyes
your beautiful legs
your soft bosom
your faithfulness
your good head

your tolerance
your warmth
your meals
your taste
and your children.
I love you
today which is Wednesday
and there's nothing we have to do
I love you at the table
at this moment
I listen to you
we talk together
you tell about a dress
oranges are lying in front of us
I love you and say so
you don't ask why
just go on talking
while I smoke my cigar.
I love you.
You take an orange from the platter
and peel it.
I bend and kiss your fingers.
They have the good smell of oranges.
I love you
and we don't have to do anything this evening.
                                    N.C./A.T.

Byron and Company

It would have been wonderful.
It's true that he really thought about it.
But it would have to be good.
Not an ordinary general store.
No mess.

The shop should be a nice one,
-not too big but suitable.
It should be in the afternoon and
the sun definitely not too
high, not too low.
And he just in shirt sleeves
and a large cravat.

The girls come by and look in.
They take three steps down and stand
in the shop and look about and
examine the bundles of kindling wood and
the sugar-loaves and the flour and cord-
age and the dried fruit and rock candy
and bay leaves and thyme and they
buy a few raisins and some powdered sugar
and ask for something he doesn't have and
giggle.

The men ask for shag.
They don't come until later.
They stand in the store alone and
their tone is matter-of-fact. As few words
as necessary, no frivolities!
Cavendish, long-spun
they'll take their pint round
the corner.

O to stretch your arms
toward the ceiling and be too tall
to go out back where to
the sun has moved
to go in and see Nelly
clover and lavender
to cross the Bosporus
through the shafts of sunlight

to be a man in shirt sleeves
who loosens his tie
to be a free man and live
with Nelly (clover and lavender)
and to hear the shop's chimes ring
with a high sound like rock candy
out there in *the shop*.

A.T.

Spring

Am I not delicious?
asks the young wife
and hangs colored eiderdown quilts
out of one window
and her breasts out of the other.

A milkman drove past
a little while ago and a
postman and I waved at them
a funeral procession drove past
with wreaths and curate
and a minister in black and I waved.

Am I not delightful?
asks the young wife
and shakes her rug
out of the window
here everybody passes by
including a man with a cow
and two boys on motorbikes
and I sent them a kiss with my fingers
and smiled.

Am I not irresistible?
asks the young wife

and springs onto the windowsill
in all her splendor.

Am I not incredible? she says
and leaps farther, landing
in a flowerbed of white narcissi.

Her husband comes home
and the bedclothes smell of sunshine
and he asks what she's doing in the flowerbed with
narcissi.

Come, you'll see, says the young wife
brushing the petals from her stomach,
it's spring.

              A.T.

Afternoon

The sun passes its zenith
and the afternoon opens up
its burned-out emptiness.

Work is suspended.

The heat summons the insects
the big and small beetles
cross each other's tracks.
The gekko's body turns
transparent in the light
and the grasshopper's wings
clatter like steel between
the leaves of the oleander.

The sea withdraws slowly,
unveiling the stones.
They pale quickly and
take on the same color as sand.

Gray, transradiated,
space spreads itself out
over the forfeited possibilities
and the tawdry dreams
of new conquests.

A B-52
from the Strategic Air Command
draws its white brushstroke
across the sky.

A.T.

Jørgen Leth
(1937)

JØRGEN LETH was educated as a journalist. He has been the organizer of text and music arrangements ("Jazz and Poetry"), a film director (special subject: representation of the myths of the sports world), and has made several television and cinema films.

He has published seven collections of poems in the years 1962–1975.

My Vietnam Poem

Notice how everything is just as it was.
We have come to know her very well.
Dazzled by her nearness we stand here watching.
She is remarkably distant although so close.
Thus, is the silence in the midst of the Music.
Thus the blue shadows in the middle of the radiant Light.
From there to there. Here I mention the word "napalm."
Napalm. Perhaps it's too trivial to tell
how she came into sight again
framed in gold and silver, surrounded by Music.
—What is your favorite color?
—What is your ideal of earthly happiness?
—What quality do you most appreciate in a man?
—What are you thinking of right now?
Perhaps it's going too far to touch on
her curious smile and the shadow in her eyes
just as the Music was starting—
and as if by magic she stood on the staircase.

234

Twelve lines before this one I mentioned the word "napalm."
Now I mention it again. Napalm. A good word.
And now comes the word "crême fraiche." And now "jealousy."
—In what way would you prefer to die?
—What are you thinking of right now?
She's not alone. She's with somebody.
We can return to that. She says something. Somebody
says something to her. She smiles. She smiles to somebody.
Thus, thus is the silence in the midst of the dizzying Music,
thus, thus are the shadows in the midst of the radiant Light.
From there to there. To there. Napalm. Crême fraiche. Jealousy.
I mention in quick succession the words
"silver," "gold," "Music," "Light," "near," "I," "words."
I say "Notice how everything is just as it was."
I say "See the latest fantastic color shots
from Vietnam."
I darken the Light and mute the Music
I won't go into
perhaps it's too lengthy to describe
her curious smile and the shadows in her eyes
as she turns to him. As she turns to him.
Jealousy. Crême fraiche. Napalm. To there. From there to there.
—What is your favorite color?
—What are you thinking of right now?
I mention in quick succession the words
"silver," "gold," "Music," "Light," "near," "I," "words."

E.M./A.T.

There Is always Music through the Walls

There is always music through the walls
always the feeling of something
going on and meaning something

you feel you are close to essential things

The arrangement
doesn't have to be changed at all
it is not in the least difficult
to orient yourself in this room
which is right in the middle of everything

Of course you can scratch your
fingers bloody on the walls
but they are where they are and the music
comes through them always

always the feeling of being
in the middle of something that means something
suspended by threads in an empty room
between walls which vibrate softly

you hear a music from other rooms
you simply can't
stop listening

you feel you are close

                                        E.M./A.T.

Tales, Number 10

But it is I who choose—to go out for example in the dark
     and take a leak
over the railing—open my door a little—be all too near. It isn't
     much to speak
of—I have tried to eradicate myself, but it was as if I were
     directed by
something or someone. I can't understand it. I can't understand it.

(Listen, in front there are trees, a hedge, asphalt)

Well, that's the way it is—for example to shout something out
     into the
air—Hell, it's I who choose—to stare out at the sea and the
     sky—to smash
this fairy tale you're telling me. It's a strange place to be.
     Much too
close. Glimpse of something strange, something fantastic. Details
     of
something unknown.

(See. In front trees, a hedge, asphalt. To the left there are
     water, trees, ships)

But why has it turned out this way? For example, to choose
     to open the door
and shut it again—to drive by in a car—yes, but isn't it I
     who choose?—
to mention beauty, scent, fabric, the natural things—to smash
your dream to pieces? I don't understand it. Why does every-
     thing look
like this? These details of something incomprehensible—I have
lost my ability to orient myself—I don't know what has become
     of my
ability to manage my everyday life.

(I repeat, in front there are trees, a hedge, asphalt. To the left
      water,
trees, ships. And to the right there's a wall and roses)

I find myself in a swamp—for example not knowing what you
      want. I don't
know what it means to choose—to look vaguely in one direction
      or another—
to stop people from getting into a car—to put my sliced-off
      hands in
your house. I have to wait and see what happens. It is im-
      possible to
come closer—I can decide for myself what I will think about—
      I can
decide for myself what I will think about—I can decide for
      myself what
I will think about.

(Now repeat to yourself, in front there are trees, a hedge,
      asphalt. To
the left there are water, trees, ships. To the right a wall,
      roses. And
in back there are some words. And behind the words silence.
      Listen,
water is trickling into a bowl. Look, the wind makes the leaves
      move)

"The sound of a clock ticking"

*Here in this boundless space there is a front, a left, a right, and
behind. And there is a back behind. There are the words, and
      there is*
the silence.

"The sound of a clock ticking" slowing fading into "the sound of a
beach"

                              E.M./A.T.

Tales, Number 15

I bend down, pick up a handful of sand and let it run through my
fingers. I don't see anything at this impossible moment and
    refrain from
saying anything about how a stranger's skin is covered with
    heather and dust.
I don't want to make a statement when first one, then the
    other, then the
third reach for their hearts. The present doesn't exist. The wind
    has died
down, you can faintly hear bygone dance music from someplace
    on the other
side. I open the door and stare out into the total darkness. Not the
sound of cars, which I suddenly long for. It is here that I can
    ask you
the common question, is there anything I can do for you?

(No, you can't do anything for me, except be here and not
    run away.)

This is an unbearable void. Not even the sound of the sea.
    The horizon
gotten rid of, I don't know whether one should worry that
    somebody crawls
groaning through the heather and tries to stand on his feet.
    It's something
I've heard about. I bend down over these hands and these
    words which are
mine for a moment. I distractedly pick up a few pretty things,
    and then
immediately drop them with casually limp wrists. Well, but
    you are porously
here, I faintly perceive that you touch my smeary walls with your
fingertips. And it is you I can ask the following real question,
    what are
you thinking about?

(I'm not thinking of anything in particular. I'm thinking about whether
    it's too late to go for a walk.)

I don't know whether it's too late. We can let the sand decide. Here, take
    a handful. Save it for later, or whatever. I'd rather stay inside anyway.
There's no sign that anybody will be a party to all that. Drink tea, wash, pay
    attention. It's possible that there is something in it. In any case, it's been
a long time since it has been this quiet. It's as if there were no world outside.
I wouldn't mind the sound of a car starting or the sound of rain. There are
    some who have said that the landscape should be investigated with the eyes,
piece by piece, and maybe shout a word into the air. It is said that something
    happens in among the bushes and trees. But now that you're here, I can ask you
directly, what do *you* think?

(I have no opinion now. I, too, think that the silence is remarkable.)

There are so many possibilities, I have some stones here that I found
    on the beach. Each one of them feels good in the hand, I place one of them
into the circle of light along with my hands and my words. Now I could go
    over to one of the bleached oak cabinets, open it, and take out my
memory of something beautiful. At least the sound of my own steps on the

floor has something to say. One could of course consider the
     matter of
opening the door and shouting words out into the silence.
     And I would
like you to feel my wrist. Another time I will ask you if *you*
     remember
something beautiful.

"The sound of a person's regular breathing"

I say everything is the same as before. I mention the beautiful
     things.
I give silence a name.

"The sound of a person's regular breathing"

E.M./A.T.

Benny Andersen
(1929)

BENNY ANDERSEN used to be a musician, playing in bars, before having a great success as a writer of children's books, radio and television comedies, and songs. His mournfully humorous poetry has by now become national property.

He has written several film scripts and widely read collections of short stories. Among his collections of poems are *Den musikalske ål* (The Musical Eel) 1960, *Den indre bowlerhat* (The Inner Bowler) 1964, *Det sidste øh* (The Last Er) 1969, *Svantes viser* (Svante's Songs) 1972, and *Personlige papirer* (Personal Papers) 1974. A selection of his poems was published by Princeton University Press in 1975.

This Uncertainty

When I at last perceived that it was certainly
not me you had said it about and it was certainly
not it you had said and it was certainly not you
who had said it I got nervous for real for what
could you now not find not to say the next time
you perhaps did not say something about me.

A.T.

Goodness

I've always tried to be good
it's very demanding
I'm a real hound for
   doing something for someone
hold coats
 doors
  seats
get someone a job
  or something
open up my arms
let someone have his cry on my shirt
but when I get my chance
I freeze completely
some kind of shyness maybe
I urge myself—do it
fling your arms wide
but it's difficult to sacrifice yourself
   when somebody's watching
so hard to be good
   for more than a few minutes
like holding your breath
however with daily practice
I have worked up to a whole hour
if nobody disturbs me
I sit all alone
with my watch in front of me
spreading my arms
   again and again
no trouble at all
I am certainly best
when I'm all alone.

         A.T.

M

Over my bed hangs a crucifix
for me love is holy
I look over my lover's shoulder
and meet the crucified one's sorrowful glance
but my lover notices
gets jealous
doesn't understand
stops
and I have to hang the Son of Man out in the kitchen
on a hook with the dish towels
but I leave the door ajar
and when we lie in a certain way I can see
my Saviour through the crack
he nods in at us: and this too I take upon me
And then when it really hurts
I get the most out of it
when it really hurts
I feel that the Thorn-Crowned
sees to it that it rightly comes to pass
that I suffer
the thorns dig into my flesh
the veil is rent from top to bottom
I bear my share of the world's suffering
it is finished.

                                                    A.T.

Photographs

She stops and pauses for breath at the landing.
All those stairs, all those years—
stands with the cold key in her hand
and listens for thieves.

Nonsense—there are only photographs in there,
good-natured, prominent eyes. ✔
No one looks like that anymore.

At last she glides through the slot
like a thin letter to herself.

A.T.

Time

We have twelve clocks in the house
still it strikes me there's not enough time
You go out to the kitchen
get chocolate milk for your spindly son
but when you get back
he has grown too old for chocolate milk
demands beer girls revolution
You have to make the most of your time while you have it
Your daughter comes home from school
goes out to play hopscotch
comes in a little later
and asks if you'll mind the baby
while she and her husband go to the theater
and while they're in the theater
the child with some difficulty
is promoted to 10th grade
You have to make the most of your time while you have it
You photograph your hitherto young wife
with fullblooded gypsyheadscarf
an opulent fountain in the background
but the picture is hardly developed
before she announces that it is nearly
her turn to collect social security
gently the widow awakes in her
You would like to make the most of your time

but all the time it stays away
what becomes of it
was it ever there at all
have you used too much time
in drawing time out
You have to make the most of time in time
roam around some time without time and place
and when the time has come
call home and hear
"Are you calling 95 94 93 92?
That number is no longer in service."
                                        Click.

                                                    A.T.

Life Is Narrow and High

A matchstick flares in space
briefly lights up a face before it dies.
In the dark hands meet
⁓ briefly touch before they stiffen.
Words are sent out.
Some few get to reach an ear
perhaps are remembered a while.
Measured lengthwise life is short
but measured vertically infinite
a quivering fiber in death's muscle.
Kiss right now
before your kiss strikes a skull.
Soon you will be no one
but now you have lips
and matches.

                                          A.T.

Earthworm

Earthnearest of all
most different from birds
sodsensitive sandticklish claylustful
you figure in no city's coat of arms
are unfit for cantatas and ads
too unheroic
too naked
your indecent intercourse with the subsoil
wakes filthy thoughts in us
which only lead us astray
but the worst is
that we are helplessly indebted to your obscene diligence
without you the globe would be sterile and void of imagination
shame on you
all of the fertile green flowering surface
is your lecherous work
and for that we will never forget you
you low underdeveloped ludicrous
lower dishonorable blunted
lowest lowestcreeping sneaking proletarian
know your place and if you dare show yourself here on the
        surface
with righteous spades we stand ready
to amputate you from yourself.

                                                              A.T.

High and Dry

The spruce saws away at the horizon
while the dunes cautiously
peep out behind one another's shoulders.
Low tide. The scowling black stones
rise up and lick their lips
with tongues of seaweed.

Pale and bitter, the lighthouse stares
at the gloating jaws of the boats—
What distant shores have they tasted—
What place could be more beautiful than this?

A dried up starfish
pointing in all directions.

                                        A.T.

Melancholy

A teaspoon lies on the road
smashed flat by a cement truck.
A window is open
but nobody looks out.
Perhaps that's why no one
puts up a ladder and elopes with
the one who isn't looking out—
or has it already happened?
It's as if everyone has gone.
In a fit of ladderlessness
I pick up the teaspoon.
Oh, how flat it's become.
I'll never come here again.

                                        A.T.

A Hole in the Earth

A hole has shown up in the earth. Empty.
Without earth around it
it wouldn't be there at all.
The hole is deeply dependent on the earth,
an emptiness that shows something exists
something that shows this emptiness exists.
If the earth wasn't there
there would be no emptiness either.
From hole you have come
to earth you shall return.
Or vice versa.
I pat the hole in a friendly way
and keep going on earth.

A.T.

Poul Borum
(1934)

POUL BORUM is an art critic and literary critic for news-
papers and periodicals. He is the editor of *Hvedekorn*, the
only magazine for young poetry in Denmark.

He has translated primarily modern American poetry and
written several film scripts and libretti for modern opera.

Among his collections of poems are *Livslinier* (Life Lines)
1962, *Mod* (Courage) 1965, *Sang* (Song) 1967, *På denne side*
(On This Page) 1970, *I live* (Alive) 1972, *Denne bog er en
drøm* (This Book Is a Dream) 1973, and *Sang til dagens glæde*
(Song to the Joy of Day) 1974.

A Green Shed

A green shed
whose scaled-off boards
shone salamander

in easter sun
near beat fields

a green shed
gathering all
the world's light

P.B.

A Train Is Passing

A train is passing
a whistle sounds
stop stop the trees cry
but it's no use
a train is passing
a sound expires
stop life cries
we are already far away
P.B.

Pictures from Reality

1
3 black horses
on 1 green field
powersun and 3
black horses

1 white sun and
1 blue sky
1 green field
and

hurry up
come and see
before everything disappears

2
On the road a bird

On the road a bird
crushed by a car
Not much left of the body
but it had open eyes

On the road a bird

3
All the leaves
on all the trees
all have totally
different motions

The sun strikes them
all the time
The wind also

4
The boy looked
at the bird
The bird looked
at the boy

Both
stiffened
Neither
moved first

                                        P.B.

Against a Wall

If you don't know what's coming
it's darkness coming.
Darkness it is, and darkness is that wall
you're standing pressed up against whispering to.
And if you don't know who's listening
it's other people listening;
they are lying listening on the other side of the wall
persuading each other they are asleep. ‑
If you don't understand where your loneliness comes from
It's from other people it comes.
Death and peace, death and peace you wish,
but you don't know what's happening,
and you receive everything in a whisper
from the others in there,
and anyway it's not death and peace you receive.
If you don't know what your life means
that's what it means.

P.B.

The Black Picture

1. I especially like the black picture.
2. It is a singular blackness you have created, sir.
3. The black picture is totally black.
4. Imagine not being able to decide where the picture stops.
5. If you perceive the black picture as a landscape the landscape is black. If you perceive the black picture as a portrait the portrait is black. In any case the black picture is an overwhelming blackness.
6. Blackness has been propagated *through* the black picture.
7. If you look long enough into your own eyes in sharp light in a mirror you see the black picture.
8. The black picture is hanging on the wall and is outside me so that I can approach it and withdraw from it, turn my back on it, kneel in front of it. I can do everything in front of the black picture.
9. It is possible to perceive the black picture as a woman and love it.
10. The blackness of the black picture asserts the illimitable. One can turn away in fright, sir. But where to?
11. What stays on the wall when you have left is the black picture, while what you take with you when you leave is the black picture.

P.B.

The House

The walls are empty of pictures now
the walls are empty
just a few fields a little lighter are outlined on the dust-gray
       wallpaper
and thin shadows of the strings
the walls are empty now

and softly the floor is yielding
tired of steps
the floor has lain down, no will any more

and on the ceiling you can read the eternally repeated geography
       of decay
these mountains and lakes only visited by occasional dying
       insects
who lived in this house? why did they leave?
was the sound of the gray door's hinges one day all of a sudden
       like a cry to them?
or were they carried out (dead or alive, crying)?

or, still simpler: where is this house?
have you seen it? have you been in it?
how is it that in an uncanny and cold way you felt at home
       there?

the walls are empty of pictures now
absence is eating you up

the poem has not yet begun

                                                     P.B.

While the House Is Burning

While the house is burning
he sits down saying:
fire is an internal phenomenon

While the house is burning
he jumps into the flames crying:
I forgot nothing in there

While the house is burning
he writes a letter saying:
tomorrow the house will burn

While the house is burning
he lies in his bed dreaming
that the house is burning

While the house is burning
he commences his dissertation:
on the metaphysical causes of fires

While the house is burning
he phones the electrician
to order new cables

While the house is burning
he realizes his defeat:
falling days, loneliness, the coming of night

While the house is burning
it turns dark in that part of the world
and he falls asleep in a strange bed

P.B.

Madrigal

Spring has come back
but I am not the same

She stands out there in the garden
her hands filled
with white and yellow flowers

But my unrest continues

Three or four clouds hover
in the shining blue sky
and the birds shoot down toward me
like arrows

Very near me
a great singing heat stands

Spring has come back
because I am not the same

P.B.

A Fierce Desire

'a fierce desire as when two shadows
mingle on a wall' — Blake

A fierce desire
as when two shadows
meet in a bright land

a moment's desire
under flapping wings
of dawn

night came to us
and complained about its loneliness
and we took unto ourselves night
we I mean I
and look night was a day in disguise

in the language of things
it is called love
but where we rule
it is called
a fierce desire

P.B.

Your Lips, Your Tongue

continue, continue, continue
          into what-
                ever
                      darkness—
                            when your skin / is there
                            there is light

and as two
moons
your eyes
            across the body's
            clear sky

you stayed long
                    between the world
and the world's shade
                    in a thin space there
        everywhere
        they had hung
memory mirrors

like a piece of green cloth
almost transparent
    the world is hanging down in front of you
and you walk into it with your eyes open

    sleep is to be recognized
    being awake is to be recognized
            being awake between sleep
            sleep dust hammered off the earth
    veins
    of hands
    like visions

who have you chosen
    as your companion
                to cross the sky?
your lips, your tongue, your lips, your tongue, continue
                                        P.B.

Inger Christensen
(1935)

TRAINED as a teacher, Inger Christensen has written a number of radio and television plays which have been presented in several countries. She is also the author of two novels as well as the two collections of poems *Lys* (Light) 1962, and *Græs* (Grass) 1963.

The connected suite of poems *Det* (It) 1969, which has united a new awareness of language with an idea of community, brought her decisive recognition, and an extraordinary great audience.

Leaning Tenderly against the Night

Leaning tenderly against the night
with the help of a rusty railing,
I find my way to my cheek and my shoulder,
I find my way to my tenderness:
iron and flesh.
              The rest are banners
silently flapping, questioning outside and inside,
in immensity of night, in immensity of mind:
                           dead?
laying my hands over the trembling face
of the night
peeling a speck of rust from my cheek.

                                  A.T.

What Is My Dead Cracked Body

What is my dead cracked body?
Ants in snow have nothing to do.
No, poetry, poetry, poetry is my body.
I write it here: what is my body?
And the ants move me, aimlessly,
away, word after word, away.

N.C.

In the Wild Mountain Solitude

In the wild mountain solitude
I draw a spruce needle carpet
over me. The dark

does not falter at the edge
presses with bristling needles
the unknown in me
opens opens

But do not grieve over me
do not grieve over your solitary
to and fro
My hour is rusty
My poem has abandoned
your well-beaten ant path
Do not grieve My young poem
is kissed more deeply by life
Deadly it creeps
over under through me
Poetry is murdered hope.

A.T.

Sorrow

Find the concise
expression for sorrow:
a black slug with slime
and reflex-mechanism
in meaningless order,
just in time the feeler is
out, just in time
pulled in again
and within the body
employed precisely
like an expectant siren
whose descending tone
descends, descends
down through the entire
organism.
O skin,
my outermost
radar screen

                                    N.C.

From: *It*

The Scene   transitivities

1

A word flies up   trying flight   Flocks
follow helter-skelter   Sturdy bio-
logical forms As if it were about security It is
about the farthest borderline   desert/not desert:

a word that flies up   flocks that follow
neither more nor less   birds that fill
this endlessly disappearing space
with an absence of explanation

It is a question of an utterly vague ex-
planation By all means hold to this explanation
Start up the wind machine and let angels with
flapping wings revolve sovereign as satellites

Let flotillas of oddly stupid creatures rush
off before the wind   insects with sails 'big and skinned   -
like lustrous illusions stand like
a vision: Being's resistance to purity

                                                S.L.F.

The Scene   variabilities

3

The one world is the only one for us
The one world is indescribable for us
Describes itself
        like imagining air above the earth
        like breath from millions of mouths
        like breath like words like screams like chemical com-
        pounds between terror of life and ter-
        ror of losing it
        this air is our only unreadable writing
        this air is our common incomprehensible work
                                conditions

        a sign a tremor clouds hoarfrost
        and we respond with tears with storms evaporations

on the way we make measurements lists statistics
on the way we take notes on each other's notes
while the writing disappears
while it rains while we write about the snow
while it snows while we write about the sun
while we weep while we laugh while we write about the
                                                    first
time we wept laughed etc. etc.

While the words storm off through the world
While I catch one here one there
necessary arbitrary   the only thing   to do
describe one confusion against the other by the other
while the sky is totally clear

                                                    S.L.F.

The Scene   transitivities

5

It should be like the feeling
It should be like the ruined summer
It should be like the chilly pause
              in the middle of a word

It should be like the feeling
It should be like a blow a relapse
It should be like the sweet relapse of forms
              into formlessness

It should be like the feeling
It should be like a denser formlessness
It should be like a tempestuous trust
              in biology

It should be like the feeling
It should be like the current fleetingness
It should be like being
                  It turned out the way it did
                                S.L.F.

The Scene   connexities

6

First and foremost the world
means something to me
I take it there are others for whom the
world means something
First and foremost the world
means something to them
Anyone else could have written this
So it surprises me that others
experience something similar
that the constructions put on the world here
others put on the world here and there
in a similar way,
that from the manifold meanings
one very simple ambiguity appears
that even the world is the same
Even the world that has no secrets
before I interfere
Even the world that has no truth
before I interfere
Even the world that finds itself in me
as the stuff we share with each other
the world itself is the same
same old stuff
we share with one another:
in itself of itself for itself

without significance
but out of itself
e.g. here where I act
as one who writes about the world
e.g. here and there where someone or other acts
as one who reads about the world
here and there and everywhere the world is
different and more than it is
like a meaningful interaction.

S.L.F.

The Scene   continuities

7

You'll find tapestries with scenes of war
stretching along the whole Maginot line

delicate prints of the Spanish Armada
floating on all the world's seas

While Potemkin on Izvestia's front page
is wrecked on a Pacific Isle

Or statues: Ivan the Terrible
smiles at the sight of Harlem

De Gaulle rides into Wenceslas Square
at the head of the red armies

and huge modern sculptures: the Chinese wall
between Spain and Spain

while Napoleon dies on Formosa

S.L.F.

Vagn Steen
(1928)

VAGN STEEN has a university degree in comparative phi-
lology. He has added a surprising and very Danish sense of
humor to poetic concretism.

He experiments with activation of readers, children's books,
television programs, newspaper reviews, and does extensive work
as an adviser in connection with the planning of new towns.

He has been a visiting professor at several American universi-
ties, and has since 1964 published a number of collections of
poems.

I Am no Shower

I am no SHOWER
don't try to turn me on
I have no faucets
don't think you can choose
among my many facets
or that I will run hot or cold
to suit your taste

but I won't go away
you will have difficulty
in turning me off

> Written in English with the
> cooperation of Rebecca Hunter

267

Technically It Is Possible

Sensations are strengthened when isolated
in the darkness my fingertips are blind
but never is their lovesong so rich
they follow your hair your skin your lines
linger on your lips eyelids
a lightning is released

I think I am nearest to you in the
sensing nearness of my fingertips
nearer I shall never come

but technically it is possible to go further
one can peel away the skin and connect electrodes
that record the fingers' journey the gradations
of temperature every beat of the artery every vein
every capillary at your little scars they stop and tell me
the ancient and exciting history of your body every
smell is recorded every little hair every grain of
dust from your fingers x-rays are sent through you your
complex of innumerable biochemicals is measured your internal
secretive life is under observation
all data are input for a highly miniaturized computer
easily inserted at my degenerate tail vertebrae
it filters adds combines has answers for everything

yet my brain is not fully automated it poses old-fashioned
questions—do you like me? I wonder breathing softly
instantly the thought is in my fingertips they glide
over you and from your data secretion pulse breath
variating local temperatures from all your data
the computer emits your answer

not a yes or a no but a series of numbers and
for purposes of dynamic description some curves

I have not learned to react frictionlessly to the
numbers but when the big day arrives our bodies
will perform a pure game a divine dialogue

—adrenaline promille 0.27
—nitrogen percentage 1.2
—pulse 120
—blood pressure 230
—pituitary gland secretion alpha 3.1765
—thigh hair¹ angle 33   •
—lip muscle tension 71
—elasticity of erection 80
—clitorial tension 67

at this moment the computer might be disconnected
but that is old-fashioned impractical
we rarely do so
unerringly it leads us further in exploring the process
it defines more positions than any Hindu manual for
limber lovers⹂ according to vitality considerations for   ˉ
weak heart muscle tensions unfavorable
blunders associations—it controls
insertion rhythm it selects appropriate words and
music—diminutive additions to the oral secretion
and special manipulations with ozonized air and
atmospheric pressure secure the cosmic experience
and the few verbal stimuli have an astonishing effect
with automatically regulated articulation
the new and very sensitive intonation regulator

it is planned to replace a number of other parts of the body
with electrodes—the technical problems have been solved
and endeavors are made to eliminate
class distinctions by producing a line of
economy limbs

as an extra added attraction for the upper class
the brain aggregate of women can be connected
- to an outlet generating continual male climax
and men to a female orgasm
complementary experiences have become a hot item
the orgasm sales catalogues list both
precise technical expressions for types

and brand names like
Cleopatra and Mary Stuart
and recently the zoologists have launched a series with
- elephant whale leopard cow eagle and sow orgasms
which require injections of additional secretions

the cheapest accessory which very soon will be standard
is a connection to poetry
the computer chooses perfectly
it synchronizes lip movements it prescribes
dosages of mood rhythm metaphors
it permutates all conceivable contact situations

but the computer generating poems verbal-thermo-
statically chosen by secretions of the body the pulse
- the breath and integrating visual excitation
and background music with additional methods of arousal
has not yet left the drawing board—the engineer seems
unwilling to stop the product development process

broadcasted coitions are still restricted to closed
circuits but amateur senders are
mushrooming—it's the hobby of the year
and more and more prerecorded coitions
can replace the concrete nearness of the body of the partner
it is simpler with tape
everybody has access to the public libraries
they have an array of the choicest classical tapes

the warehouses stock tapes by top performers
people swap tapes like mad children steal
and senior citizens in rest homes gorge themselves
replaying old tapes

today we have reached nearly total security
against miscodings and short circuits in the computer
and some publishers—but still too few give
unconditional guarantee of workmanship and durability

Mirror Mirror on the Wall

MIRROR MIRROR
                    ON THE WALL
WHO'S THE WHO'S THE
                    –ST
          OF THEM ALL
                    V.S.

$a$capitalistic$society$

$a$capitalistic$society$
counts$everything$in$money$and
$capitalizes$all$services$every-
thing$gets$a$monetary$expression$
iscounted$precisely$everything$
hasa$monetary$aspect$everything$
                    V.S.

Hans-Jørgen Nielsen
(1941)

AFTER having studied literature at the University, Hans-Jørgen Nielsen has worked as a critic for Copenhagen newspapers with a more and more marxist orientation.

He is coeditor of various literary and music magazines, organizer of happenings, and philosophic originator of the so-called "attitudinal" relativism.

In his novels, essays, and poems 1965–1972 he has made use of a variety of styles.

Mobiles. Variations on the Snow

1
the snow is snow
and it snows
the snow is snow
and it writes
the writing is snow
and it writes
the writing is snow
and it snows
the snow is writing
and it snows
the writing is writing
and it snows
the snow is writing
and it writes

the writing is writing
and it writes

2
   a snow that
is moving

a snow that
is moving
like a snow
that is moving

that is moving
like a snow

       ✿

   a snow that
is standing still

a snow that is standing still
like a snow
that is standing still

that is standing still
like a snow

    ✿

a snow is standing still
a snow is moving

a snow is everywhere

snow crosses my mind:
                                        snow
            I say
here in this place
        snow remained hanging in the air:
                                        ·then
            fell flakingly
here in this place
        here where it's been snowing then
                                        but
            hasn't been snowing
here: in this place
                                        T.Ø.

The Body, A Burning Singing-machine

it's in the air   it's stirring
smoothly   anytime this fire
may be inserted   and
in his body the thrushes of whiteness
are released by geometrical fountains

here something comes into the picture   here
something creeps into
the body   anywhere the fire may spread
and burn through the paper   as
the thrushes of whiteness in his body
are released by geometrical fountains

here they're lighting a fire that means
nothing   here they're lighting a fire that

glows   anything's in the air
and stirring devouringly   anything's
spread out glowing   and
by the fountains of whiteness are released
geometrical thrushes in his body

it means nothing   it means
here's a fire that's
stirring   anytime it may all
burst   anytime he may
step out of his flesh   as
geometrical thrushes are released
in the body of whiteness by his fountains

here something appears in a new light   here
something else comes into
the picture   anywhere it may turn up
and insert itself in the flesh   anywhere
a flesh may give way and make room
for the fire   as
the geometrical thrushes in his body
are released by the fountains of whiteness

it's a fire that's slowly swerving
about   ᵗit's a flesh that's slowly giving
way   anything's stirring
devouringly   anything may swerve into
an unknown flesh   as
fountains of thrushes are released
by the whiteness in his geometrical body

here's the place where the fire is   here where
the place is the fire is   anytime
it may creep back into the empty
air   anywhere it may lose itself

in an unknown flesh or
in anything   just as
geometrical whiteness is released
by his fountains in the body of thrushes

T.Ø.

A Few Lines and a Dog

Outside is the world or inside is the world. And 'the world'
may be a few lines a dog goes past.

  The dog is either 'inside' or 'outside.' That
rather depends on how you see it.

  Inside outside is 'the world' or else it is outside
inside. 'The world' is there anyhow
isn't it?

Now the dog is gone. Nothing's left but the lines.

T.Ø.

From:
The Figures, Moved in Their Images

Not only her

    not only her
      but also the way she smiles
  & not only the way she smiles
      but also the way she is present
  & not only the way she is present
      but also her hand
  & not only her hand by itself
      but also her hand in his hand

    & not only her hand in his hand
        but also his hand in her hand
    & not only his hand in her hand
        but also his hand by itself
    & not only his hand
        but also the way he is present
    & not only the way he is present
        but also the way he smiles
    & not only the way he smiles
        but also him

                              T.Ø.

A Picture Somewhere in Language

1

IT'S LATE IN THE DAY
THEY COME RUNNING ALONG THE ROAD
SHE HAS 'LONG FAIR HAIR
HE'S LOOKING AT HER LONG FAIR HAIR
AS THEY COME RUNNING

2

you may call it a picture
it's just not a real picture
it's a picture in language
but because it's LATE IN THE DAY
the picture is actually grayish white

somewhere in this grayish white picture
THEY come running
and later it appears from the picture
which is just a picture in language
that they are HE and SHE

from the picture it also appears
that it's her long fair hair HE

is looking at as THEY come running
they come running along the road
and HE'S LOOKING AT HER LONG FAIR HAIR

certain things suggest that the long fair hair
is hanging loose as SHE comes running
along the road in the grayish white picture
then the long fair hair is probably flowing
as HE's looking at it in language

and THEY don't run in language they COME RUNNING
along the road in the grayish white picture
and that is important although this picture
probably means nothing more
than what it is

it's just LATE IN THE DAY
they just come RUNNING ALONG THE ROAD
she just has LONG FAIR HAIR
and he's just looking AT HER LONG FAIR HAIR
AS THEY COME RUNNING

3
if you step back
the black invades the white
and makes it grayish white
you have to call it A PICTURE

but it's not a REAL PICTURE
it's just a picture IN LANGUAGE
and this picture in language is GRAYISH WHITE
but not just because it's late in the day

the black invades the white
and somewhere in the black comes a her
and she has long fair hair which IS HANGING LOOSE
and probably FLOWING

maybe that's what throws a shadow
into the white and makes it grayish white
and it's important that she DOESN'T RUN there
IN LANGUAGE in the grayish white picture

it's important that she comes running there
as she throws her shadow into the white
in the picture which is not A REAL PICTURE
but where black and white merge into GRAYISH WHITE

black and white merge IN LANGUAGE into grayish white
as she DOESN'T RUN with her long fair hair
which IS HANGING LOOSE and probably FLOWING
but comes running there along the road

and THAT IS IMPORTANT ALTHOUGH THIS PICTURE
PROBABLY MEANS NOTHING MORE
THAN WHAT IT IS they come running
and he's looking at her long fair hair.

                                                            T.Ø.

On the Verge of Poetry

One evening in 1856 Karl Marx is suddenly on the verge
of poetry: "As I cannot kiss
with my lips, I must kiss with my tongue
and make words. Indeed, I might even make verse"
he writes in Manchester, in an unfamiliar room.

The words are addressed to Jenny
who isn't there.

But she's passionately present
as an absence,
an empty space hallucinated among the excerpts
from the political economists.

"I've got so far that I'll be through
with all that economic shit in five weeks"
he wrote to Engels, one spring day,
but that's five years ago now.

Where there's shit
you can count on golden heavens.

Tonight he makes love alone with the ink, obsessed
with 'the charm of distance,'
the poetical tongue gorging itself
with language in the economy of absence and want.

T.Ø.

Per Kirkeby
(1938)

PER KIRKEBY is a poet, painter, and natural scientist (geologist). He is also the organizer of happenings and editor of various magazines. He has as a geologist participated in several expeditions in Greenland.

Apart from having been the coauthor of a travel account from Mexico, he has published a number of texts (1966–73) with affinities to American pop art.

From: *Explanations of Pictures*

1. Through Central Park early afternoon in the beginning of
        December
without any violent experiences. Shocking: the rock is sticking
        up. Or
trees partly leafless (the rest yellow) and fir trees and worn
        lawns
somewhere between ochre and faded green. This also goes for
        the light
but that might be because it is oblique. Round the skyline
        of Manhattan
which—especially when I look downtown—appears like a moun-
        tain landscape
(yes, there is no getting round it) a distant mountain landscape a
little bluish gray of hue. In the park are beautiful blue birds and
many big unsuspicious gray squirrels.

2. Serious man with long tight-fitting legs surrounded by yellow
light. He is: scarlet, orange, and pink. He is accompanied by
        irregular

(because of clouds) circle symbol containing an American
        eagle with
its wings spread,

3. 4 blue lines arranged round a square but so that they do
        not quite
meet. They try.

4. A strange figure—seen from the back?—in a cowl?—But he
        has a
yellow section down his—back? and black spots, clothes-shadows
        and
orangeearth-shade. But is it a man? The figure is in fact
        accompanied
by a circle symbol, very meticulously, but a very beautiful lioness.

5. Plastic circle symbol: far-off soft night sky. The circle in the
circle is the red moon, dangerously close. The white palms
        are moved in
a ghostly way by the night wind—Miami and South Pacific.

6. The blue girl whose hair the nightwind of the palms is playing
with. The silver shoes become pink in this light. Space vi-
        brating in
dark green.
7. The house: rectangular with an opening of columns at one
        end—all
types of columns are acceptable. Obviously white outside and
        blue inside.

                                                    P.B.

From: Jüngling auf der Wanderschaft

A swift little shower standing obliquely over the open country
just gets the grass of the country moistened
and the sun shines again over the open country
over the open country a wind is rising
and the wind from heaven over the open country
makes the Chinese straws wave toward the ground
and the wind and the sun together dry the grass of the country
but the glittering drops are hidden in the wood
dripping from the leaves' roof on the plants of the forest floor
      in the faded cover of leaves
here are neither sun nor wind with their draining power
intertwined leaves and boughs make up the green valve of
      the wood
sunlight sifting in thin stripes through the valve of the wood
makes golden spots that are messengers from a brighter world
      on the floor of the wood
from the open country the wind is rumbling against the wood
      in vain
toward the draining wind of the open country the beach lowers
      big boughs
and join together hazel sloe hawthorn
the wood turns its needle fir toward the draining grass of the
      open country
and the waving straws in front of the wood are calm
only the green valve rocking vaguely in the wind from heaven

                                   P.B.

From: Jüngling auf der Wanderschaft

two naked women with long black hair
caryatids with two naked women
with heavy silver ornaments round the naked necks of
two naked women with transparent drapings
with long vertical lines down the naked hips of
two naked women with dark pubic hair
between the naked legs of two naked women
with naked breasts on two naked women
somewhat smaller the naked Jesus
with drapings round the naked legs of
the naked Jesus who shows his perforated palms
behind the naked Jesus two naked women
with drapings over the naked bodies
around the black hair of the naked women is a golden light
wild wings are growing from the backs of the naked women
in the solitary landscape the sky is rather dark
solitary rock formations stick out from the plateau
where only a few solitary trees are standing
they have all disappeared into the smallest house
the street is utterly empty and the windows of the house
        are empty
the sun is shining on the empty house

P.B.

From: 2 Poems

an obscure light enveloping a woman sharp light from an
        unscreened bulb throwing light radiating over a woman's
        hair shoulder the top side of the breasts one hand
        turned up
a gray light drawing, granular and sharp, a woman's profile
a dress of gray-flecked wool
a cropped woman
among skyscrapers fog and over it an airplane
in a gray light a shining car 36
in falling snow and under a clouded sky a sailing ship between
        icebergs and steep dark rocks
a man filling the radiator of an old bus
a man with a big bushy moustache sitting at the gray light
        of a window
in an obscure light an almost naked woman with her hair
        taken up and a gentleman in an elegant suit
a sharp light and strong shadows drawing the ornamented
        façade of a palace
in black outlines a statue of a warrior with a raised sword
        against the drifting clouds
in a slanting light eight men lying with their guns behind a
        low rampart across a street
children playing on an uncut lawn between low building blocks
big gray clouds across a broad wet street with three streetcars
        and only a few pedestrians
a man with two big spanners and on a field a row of tractors
at a roadside a row of people were standing behind a long
        row of racing cyclists
a gigantic building with points and spires and a strong light
        on one side beyond a dark city
flowering orchards and a shallow river without a ripple
three fishermen in a boat on a river with big fir trees on
        the banks

a palace lying in strong slanting light and the statues of an
    entrance drawing long black shadows across a road
eyes like amber and seaweed and green under an ocean surface
low sunrays striking a house in front of a white sky
trucks on a road
morning light striking flowery wallpapers
gulls in front of the ocean haze
a young man with distant eyes and his left hand in a wistfully
    beseeching gesture on his breast
the ocean rolling toward a rocky beach while glassy puddles
    are purple
a naked woman on a terrace sprawling in the morning sun
    with a cup in her left hand
in front of closed shutters and heavy drapings a woman lying
    in a black dress with big wings
a naked woman on a stormy rock island fire from her raised
    hand is pale against the morning light a gull with
    its beak open across the rock island
a woman on a road

P.B.

Henrik Nordbrandt
(1945)

HENRIK NORDBRANDT has studied Oriental languages at the University of Copenhagen. He has lived for long periods in Turkey and Greece. He has translated and adapted Turkish poems and tales into Danish. He has published six collections of poems 1966–1974.

Disconnection

streets
under me
over me
around me
tunnels
railway tracks
conduits
between points
ready to leap

the trains have stopped
people have stopped
blood has stopped

can we manage
trapped in metal

death lurks in the electrical contacts
can we set it in motion
with a blow of the hand

will it then
strike through us
like a complete photograph
of broken connections

N.C./A.T.

Stairsong

your face
in the evening
a slowly
burning phonograph record

you arranged the fragrances of the vestibule
in vases of dust
placed your instruments meticulously
in the tuning forks of the light

lavender and camomile
oboes and violins
a pattern
on the well-worn carpets

just when the light was
reasoning with your face
you put your mouth
to the stairwell

and sang me up
to your closed door

N.C.

German Soldiers' Graves

now the skeletons lie exposed
on the border between mould and clay, like split
hearts in open wounds. if they still

beat, they are heard only by moles
by blind moles and insect larvae
hibernating for the winter.

and for the sake of your diary, Liebchen,
i note that the sun is about to go down. october
leaves fall, you would say, like a gentle funeral march.

but there is also another sound. of earth
dropped down into earth, a resonance-box of earth
laid in circles of earth. minds which understood nothing

have become their own answers. reassuring:
a thin husk of bone
divides us from metaphysics.

N.C.

To a Death Mask

you are a child of your own sleep and therefore sleepless.
for your sake wanderers on the glass-mountain slope never
find rest, the bird never finds its way back to its nest
and the wind in the prayer wheel repeats your words in a
ceaseless
cradlesong that keeps you awake. you are set like a door
in the opening which dreamers go through when they wake
but through which you yourself are never allowed to pass.
you are a child of those who sleep and for their sake eternally
sleepless.

N.C.

When a Person Dies

When a person dies
his surroundings remain behind:

The mountains in the distance
the neighborhood houses
and the road that on Sunday
leads over a wooden bridge
on the way out of town.

And the spring sunshine
that rather late in the afternoon
reaches a shelf of books
and magazines which undoubtedly
were once new.

It's not a bit strange.

But all the same it has
often surprised me.

N.C.

Anaesthesia

In a decaying park

delayed voices
growing more distant

in marble that will
never be completely

conscious of itself.
N.C.

Baklava

I feel uneasy in Athens, Istanbul,
and also in Beirut. People there
seem to know something about me
which I never understood,
something enticing and dangerous
like the underwater grave rows
where we dove for amphorae last summer,
a secret—half sensed
in the street vendors' glances—which suddenly
make me aware of my skeleton.
As if the gold coins the children
hold out toward me
were stolen from my own grave
last night. As if they had casually
crushed every bone in my head
to get at them. As if
the cake I just ate
were sweetened with my own blood.

N.C.

Byzantium

Woodsmoke drifts away over the sunken graves
     and the winter evening's waning light
reaches a limit where only death-sentenced faces are strong
                             enough
     to muster sufficient resistance.
Women calling out into the darkness from the open doors of
                            dilapidated houses
     try to tell me something
which the children, who reluctantly cease their play in the
                            ruined church,

do not understand. And throughout the night
black stallions with bloodshot eyes run wild in the narrow streets
    when, from the sound of their hoofbeats,
they sense that the riders in silver-studded saddles died a long
           time ago.
           N.C.

In an Asian Village

How difficult to name things
    in the right order:
The cracked mud walls, which come into sight
    behind the blossoming peach trees at
           afternoon prayer time
when one descends from the mountains in the east
    and the sound of children's voices, which suddenly become
           still
in the bamboo forest on both sides of the road ...

How difficult to say
    which of the things came first ...

The blossoming peach trees in the sunshine
    or the traveler, who descends from the mountains
        in the east.

The song, or the things
    which force it to be sung.
           L.T.

A Funeral Portrait

Wondering, we held you up in the sunlight
and wiped the dust from your face.
With an expression like a wounded traveler
who one spring day just at evening
arrives at a little village in the mountains
and dies, without having been able to tell
who he is, and where he comes from
—thus your image spoke to us.
Your mouth tried to express something
which we ourselves had always wanted to say
and your eyes observed a landscape
which we ourselves had always longed for.

As if the uncertainty of your fate
with those, whom you left long ago
and the uncertainty of your genesis
with those, who laid you in your grave
made you an object for a conjecture
whose unformulated, half-surmised words
united the first with the last in us
when we held you up in the light again.
And when we wiped the dust from your face
we didn't know who it was
who touched you with our hands:
Whether it was those whom you left
who again caressed you, in longing
or whether it was those whom you died among
who again touched your corpse, in anxiety.

—All that we knew, O traveler
was that we felt compelled to destroy you again.
And like the soldiers who left you behind
wounded in the mountains, we wounded you once more

with broken bottles and fag-ends of cigarettes
before we shattered you with our rifle butts
and burned down the chapel where we found you.

                                                          A.T.

Civil War

The moon cannot find
what it came to shine on.
Whitewash has flaked off the houses.
The riverbed has run dry.
And the young widows have forgotten
how to look up.

                                                          N.C.

Dan Turèll
(1946)

DAN TURÈLL is a bilingual Copenhagen cosmopolitan. He has, for instance, translated T. S. Eliot, Allen Ginsberg, and William Burroughs. He is also a diligent contributor to the "underground" literature of the young generation.

From: Karma Cowboy Theme Song

Some folks got to reason
Oh but I hope you'll understand
I don't reason nothin' I'm just
ridin' thru the land
ridin'
ridin' thru the land
writin'
daybreak thru my hand

The Karma Cowboy
is only a tool
in the hands of a Karma
that makes him a fool

He'll go upside-down
and back 'round the bend
He'll see Death Mouth eating
each postcard you send

He plays the act
he knows how to play

He says the things
he's got to say
He rides around
from town to town
just full-time turnin'
upside-down

He got no plan
Got no idea
He may not be
'not even here'
But as the wind
and smoke may dance
you'll see him move
by simple chance

He has to die
some other day
That's just to live
some other way
And as they take him
out of sight
a voiceless voice
says 'it's all right'

From: Song for Blake

In darkness of winter
He's singin' his tune
Singin' cold winter into
Another sweet June

Singin' thru the flesh
Singin' thru the bones
Singin' from the oceans
And the many-colour'd stones

Singin' like some birdie's call
Sounding here and not at all
Singin' of Eternal Love
Singin' here yet high above

Singin' of the Doors
That always should be clean
Singin' of that Infiniteness
Everything would mean

Singin' thru the light years
Right thru the smoke of Time
That pure and fleshly Human Song
Shall be the end of human crime

Canto XXXVII

'There is no escape, Count Dracula ... Even YOU
can not stand before the FIRECROSS!'

'e just come out o' the sea, 'e did ...
caught 'im blinkin' dead ...
Too late for the Doc anyway'

> This Cold Lifeless Body
> UNDEAD
> UNLIVING
> changes shifts alters
> its very form itself
> faster than the human eye
> can follow

'A transfusion of blood
through the dark clinging shadows
... Look at his e-eyes
Burning
Burning –'

Flashing hours ... Closing time
on a cold winter's night
such as this ... The scream echoes
in the swelling darkness and then
abruptly fades ...

Creatures of the Dead
flowing in the shadows of the night ...

the Hand of Mindless Terror
through the soundless mist ...

Canto XLVI

'DEATH
rides the rails'

. . . downwards
through the early morning skies

pick-up Death
by my hands . . .

Faster
Ever faster
The cleansing trance rays
So many times
Before

' – I will allow no one
to enter . . . No one,
Herr Dracula'

' – There is no such thing
as 'Safety,'
Monsieur . . . no
such thing'

Elsewhere
on this only railroad:

His face fixed
like a Death-mask
through the narrow mind corridors
so many times

INSTANTANEOUS FINAL DEATH
in the eyes of Doc Sun

'– *And should you fail . . .'*

'*That scream* – ?'

'KEEP THE DOORS LOCKED!'

'He's already gone . . .
Just a thin wisp
of smoky mist
slithering past
the metal brain rooms – '

Outside State
at this hour
'*Traced me . . .*
This Late Night . . .'
Cold cracks . . .
Across the empty
metal tracks . . .
A score to settle
with you
'Human Form'

Clutches of Madness
OVER
  and
    OUT

Peter Laugesen
(1942)

PETER LAUGESEN was trained as a typographer. He is strongly influenced by revolutionary French poetry. The Danish translator of Artaud, he has written a series of "fleets" about the creative process.

Manuscript 4th Version

Different landscapes and ways of experiencing them.
Lost things are on their way to a new writing.
Movements are experienced and overcome.
Necessities disappear where I am a part of things.
My motives are reaching out for places where the pointed
       remains are deposited.
The raw material of writing is without connection with the ocean.
Poetry and the wordings are wrenched from each other.
I eliminate the acquisitions.
That is a movement.
Destruction led out over the edge where something is moving.

The word flower is crazy.

Anthony felt her presence her breath reached him from the
       corner of her mouth. Soon they were lying together
       down at the beach.

In perhaps identical fields the beings exist.
We are forced to new expansions.

I do not seek in the asphalt of main roads.

An outline was hiding the lower part of the sky where a
   street would otherwise have run to.

P.B.

November Piece

The color of the music is the blowing and sloping
landscape so thin that it seems that only the surface exists,
the terminal, the conquering grayish street.

In the intervals one looks into abysses, there is no peace,
no stopping. The sound of falling goats gets out to you, the
soughing and the crying, nailed and tied to a ladder, with a
white view.

The biting slow ties keeping hold of your limbs,
where you are hanging.

The wood turns away in an arch down into a night still
more horrible than civilization has made it, full of people and
things with human qualities.

The thick smell is everywhere in the clouds and is only
dissolved in the grass in the morning, in that sad moment when
everything is beautiful. Day does not at all come into the
picture at any time.

P.B.

From: Writing

By writing a writing I make another writing more important

snow no longer keeps its connection with hand

time has coiled up into words

Some images come back others I have to fetch back

The stones are shining in the leveled city

The buildings are not signs here

    The road is absolutely empty in the rain the
skilled movements do not change it

    the territory is oozing intervals sentences
are already running over the soil

    the streets are not connected daily life is in some other
quarter

a diagram of poetry's triumphal procession back through the
        future

I do not believe the landscape can become a higher degree of
image nor that the sentence can become any higher

    the writing is still looking for places where a little of
it can be without getting the character of writing

I choose
        a special poetry for the unusable

A mixture of things fleeting sloping landscapes the spots in
the sun the spots in the snow the houses are wet

> I do not remember the place does not seem to have changed
> very
much the writing does not look as changed as I do the names
are telling
themselves a special direction I experience it as names

> it will be just a moment then the reliving is ready to follow

I never write anything that isn't a letter for you. The next day
the flower was in the writing

I am writing the places the same place

The back of the paper doesn't exist

P.B.

From: Catatonia

They slid along the shining black mirror restlessly
She felt the weight of her limbs as after the construction of life
She hardly noticed the expanse of the black surface and
didn't see that it colored the eyes of both of them
Black mirrors are reflecting black mirrors
eyes impenetrable
  eyes impenetrable
Her hands were not where they should have been
space was madly shrunken
and the head she loved so much grinned from the stake
while nothing was going on any more in the glazed eyes
With a cry she threw herself through the mirror
and doesn't feel that it is no longer there

that the cry ceases on its way
through the vanished black mirror
She hardly notices what's happening
and when she looks around she doesn't know
where she is
She doesn't recognize the picture wall behind her back
the filled sounds
She doesn't know the saturated heavily colored air
through which her body is moving
                    the
                imperturbably
             meaningless dialogue
              moves rapidly
           through his head while god
          is raising up roaring half a
          meter behind him
The street splashed over with rain
makes impressions on her mobile body
He is drawing his feet
through what he receives
She is swimming through the red liquid
with her eyes hidden behind curtains of tears
and all the time the black mirror and his distorted face
can just be seen on the bottom

                                              P.B.

From: It's only a Paper Moon

I can hardly see you
I can hardly see you
I can hardly see you

The houses are opening their eyes but
of course that is something
I imagine of course
it is ridiculous to ontologize
the houses

Let us take a walk in the garden
talk together

The moon is a big dark
chunk of materials which
like a ball moves roundly
through space together with the earth
and at the same time moves
around it
The moon is rolling over the ocean
like you rolling on my back

Here
the trail
ends

Here
many trails
begin

                                                    P.B.

From: I Can Hear You Singing

I have written a lot
about the revolt and
afterwards forgotten all of it
What is really happening
Here are the sounds a pen
a guinea-pig eating
a snowplow on the road
the endless seething in my ears
Here are some books some notes
the sound of a cigaret burning
of a violin lying in its box
of snow melting on the floor
coffee slowly evaporating in the cup
a bird changing its position in the cage
a table red like a memory
a storm that disappeared yesterday
I let beauty turn in
before putting pen to paper
the fairy tale is so disturbing
what world is it I am writing
I can hardly remember anything
the sounds are not going to die
I love you but there is no way
of telling you

P.B.

From: Divine Innocence

What Artaud is
Is perpetual dissecting
Cutting laying bare to
Find Real Things in the
Whole fantastic
Pattern of phenomena and
Events which is
Artaud's writing cuts
Through the veil of conscience

Phonetic scalpels
Grammatical knives
Syntactical sounds
Coldly and sharply
In through the vanishing
Point

The Absolute in everybody
The Absolute in everything
The Absolute in all
The Absolute
Absolutely

Cooking a grin full of gravel
Cooking a grin full of pebbles
Cooking a grin full of seaweed
Cooking a grin full of sharp
Beautifully arranged stones

P.B.

Rolf Gjedsted
(1947)

ROLF GJEDSTED has translated Baudelaire, Georg Trakl, and Rimbaud. He has also done radio and publishing work.

From 1969 to 1975 he has published six collections of poems.

Old Water

Under white vaults
I heard whispering water—
or did the wine make me too sensitive?
in this white house
a strong, dark tree shot up
through the splintered floor
and the chalked water.
Under the wedding stairs
of gold & ice
my love & I gazed at
a rare mosaic:
opal skies spread with
great turquoise tears
& silver angels, who held up heaven,
& angels screaming out the silence of gods
over a dizzying abyss.

R.G.

Dawn

Just arose from my birth
with my head upside down
(like a crucifixion)
with all future feelings
gripped in each hand/
deaf & blind,
ready for perfection,
ready to set the heart going,
ready to consume all liquids
& let my skin dry in the wind
& rub away the pictures/
already dying
at my mother's breast
black sorrow sweeps past
like an electric cat.

               R.G.

Rain

Birds do not hatch out eggs
man has touched,
they throw them into the ocean
or crush them on stones ...
I lose myself in the water.
As deep as high above it
the sky looks like rain ...

               R.G.

Insanity

It is not possible to sit alone in a park, eating a meal of fresh
fruit & wine! Each movement is followed by suspicious eyes!
And if you actually should jump up, screaming at the top of
your voice, nobody would be surprised...

Every day a woman is sitting on a bench in the park with her
dog, she lets it drink from the fountain...The woman is mad
...The dog is a toy dog! Grownups laugh with the children,
to let her know that she's mad.

They jump out from the paths. And on her way through the
park they throw stones at her (as if she were a blackbird)...

I SHALL NEVER SPREAD MY LEGS & WITH A CRY LET
A CHILD KICK ITS WAY OUT THROUGH MY WOMB...
R.G.

Salt

As for the possessed, moments occur
when his senses are sharpened to the utmost,
there will be hours for the deeply drugged
when he will catch the colors of sexes
& hear the tune of salt...
After deep sleep he sees truths
by crossing a street,
by eating a fruit etc...
He is attacked by shadows from harried houses
in the oldest part of town...
With this consciousness it is even more beautiful
& twice as painful
to be witness to greater connections,
like the restlessness of watches,
or the rotation of the earth...
R.G.

Sten Kaaløl
(1945)

STEN KAALØ is an actor, poet, and translator of English drama.

He has published a novel about his generation, *Skønne dage* (Wonderful Days) 1974, short stories, and three collections of poems whose distinctive mark is the playful, erotic, and humorous tone.

For Ever

after having waited one late afternoon in August
in the town of Tomelilla
after having walked past the station's rest room
that whispered to me
after having ordered coffee
at Ingeborg Larsson's coffee shop across from the station
after having played the Bee Gees'
"Don't forget to remember me" for 50 öre
on Tomelilla's only scarlet jukebox
after having watched the chandelier there on the ceiling at
        Ingeborg's
after having kissed the side of her fish tank in the corner
after having smiled at Ingeborg who smiled
after having smoked two John Silvers
after having filled out a coupon in the newspaper
after Tomelilla's Hell's Angel had come into the coffee shop
with his girl friend
after he had thrown my cream into the fish tank
after I had gotten up and thought of throwing him in the
        same direction
after I had walked out onto the sidewalk over to his
White chrome-plated Harley Davidson

after I had pretended to piss on it
after I had disappeared from the Angel's range of vision
after I had gone into the rest room in the station
after I had read all the names and declarations of love
and after I had also written a little greeting
after I had peed
after I had heard and seen someone take hold of the door
          handle
after I had held a long whispered conversation with the toilet
          bowl
about poetry in general
after I had sat down on the train again
and had ridden a few stations
in she comes one girl or another
into the compartment
and the train is still waiting to pull out after she has gotten on
and the chance is there
suddenly I can just take it
          jump up
       and grab her by the hand
              and jump off
                  and rip off a neat little car
and then it's her and me for ever
one girl or another
but nothing happens
and she/her name is already Anita
she of course sits right across from me right across from me
even though there are lots of other seats
sits down and smiles like a second Harriet Andersson
at any rate with a Swedish expression around the corners of
          the mouth
and the train is already pulling out
     We could have been halfway to Poland now
        seen the sun go down over the mountains of Krakow
          made love in the dark in Warsaw
             found ourselves in the middle of the Eastern Bloc

and then it would've been her and me for ever
one girl or another
but nothing happens
and now it's too late really
but I can still just make it
she digs up a complicated book out of her basket
and now's the time to move over to her:
  that man Sartre his philosophy and all that stuff
    why don't we get off at the next stop
  I know a hotel in Poland for instance
    or Prague or Budapest
      I know a whole lot
        We could go to a hotel
          and kiss each other
and then it's us two you and me for ever
one girl or another
but nothing happens
and a long time afterwards/Anita jumps off at the last second
and hurries across the platform in the rain
it's impossible to react
  she's already in the hall of the railway station
    with the hotel room halfway into the wastepaper basket
      she's already sitting in the taxi
        and asking for a light in Warsaw
          she's already in her kitchen
            and peeling the Eastern Bloc
and it was her and me for ever
one girl or another
but nothing happened

                                                          L.T.

You Sit out there, Peeing

I cover the door with kisses
the sky above the land is shiny as a porcelain sink
the trees are dripping
I kiss your shoulders of birds' wings
the street lamps topple over, extinguished in the piles of red
          leaves
the last wet dandelions of summer solidify
I kiss your thighs of living cats
behind the town, the laundry is burning on kerosene clotheslines
piano music sounds form an apartment in Landskrona
I kiss the snowfall in your light auditory canals
you sit out there, peeing
a bride and groom float by, high above the forest
the booksellers rush out on the street
I kiss the soft orchards/pollen-filled groves in your eyes
a freshly painted train arrives steaming hot at the station
like an opened vein from inside the town
I kiss your soaked elbows/classical music/orange scent
the great troll walks across the landscape, burdened by autumn
well-disguised in dry cool beachsand
I kiss your lymph nodes of drenched green moss
you sit out there, peeing
a fuzzy stag wants money from all the banks handed over
it wants it in a light hind
I kiss your crotch of cold salty crabmeat
the earth wipes off its strawberry spit under the houses
the red rustling beech leaves creep toward your soapbreasts
I kiss your buzzing nipples of loose velvet springs
the sky rains wood lice
the sand troll runs through my closed hands
I kiss your backside of coke and faience
you sit out there, peeing
a grand piano rises in the air above Landskrona
the stag comes out of the banks with its light hind

I kiss your filled tomato-burst lips/the trees tumble down
you're lifted up between the tiles and the cisterns and make
       a turn over the Sound
by wireless I have your blazing lungs in my knees
I kiss your closely written feet of thin white paper
and by the church facing Humlebæk on the isle of Hven
you sink slowly and shining downward without underpants
I kiss you under your dress like a cream-wasp in raspberry
       powder
you sit out there, peeing
and as through an aching green tarsal bone
you arrive like a marmoset at Tycho Brahe's Observatory
I kiss each and every charcoal gray mole and lick each and
       every worm
a troll shows you around the stars
a little red blood gushes out of your anus
I kiss your muscle of shiny dewy metal
and out under the eaves I see you flying in the rain of insects
you smile without underpants like milk on its way out of a cow
I kiss you/put you in my mouth until you crunch like a wing
and the luminous grand piano begins to snow red like a hospital
you get cold like a smashed muskox between the clouds
I kiss your empty underpants on the doorknob →
lick you warm on the field between your eyes
I cover the door with kisses
you sit out there, peeing

                                         L.T.

Run

today I feel rotten
I wish I were a handrail in Brazil
                 that just thought about the wind and rain
and my love
whom today incidentally I love more than ever before
detests me
and turns her lips north-south
if I come running east-west
today I feel rotten
       I am a massacred French horn in the royal orchestra
       I am a bent-over figure on the beach from a film
I wish I were a handrail in Brazil
                 that just thought about the wind and rain
and not instead this chain-smoking morning's reconciliation
on a marathon-like run after my love's lips
north-south
east-west
I feel rotten today

                                   L.T.

Recollection

the family lying on a woolen blanket—
faded blue checks between their naked bodies—
the grass dry
the house quiet in the afternoon light
my wife asleep
I go into the living room to get something
inside it is cool and dark
the windows open
a spoon falls from the dish drainer
white powder all over the dresser
clover
last night everything was wet
I write it down
a cow gets up

L.T.

Lean Nielsen
(1935)

L EAN NIELSEN grew up in a working-class district in Copen-
hagen. The motifs of his poetry are taken from everyday
real life, which he represents with a firsthand social engagement,
poetry of a narrative, almost novelistic character.

From 1969 to 1974 he has published five collections of poems.

Kurt's Story

Kurt had raped
a minor

his nature was gentle
evasive and humble
he was mentally backward

he was often bullied
by the rest of us
cut off from any close relations

we often beat him up
forced him to eat earthworms
humiliated him and brought him to tears
felt ever so noble
when now and then
we allowed him to listen
and never touched him

once he ran away from the Home
and never came back

one of our teachers
said he'd been taken

to a Home for the mentally deficient.
                                        K.H.

Brothers Meet

I was never good at begging
for public assistance, nor in the streets,
that's why I have always
noticed people with a knack for that

sat with my beer
when a gentleman with a meager melancholy face
sat down opposite me
and he asks me for a beer

he seems to have had a few.
tells me about divorces
long illness, sick pay, social security,
and now and then his eyes fill with tears
we have two beers together
while I listen, powerless as always,
think of giving him ten bob,
but gold dust never weighed me down,
so I settle for just five
and get up and leave

wander about along the canals
enjoy the shapes of the boats, the old houses,
the trees, the spire of Our Saviour's
while his sad account now and then
glides past behind my brow

on my way home
I see my friend leaning against a house,
he comes toward me
and asks can I spare a few bob
I bloody just gave you five.

forgotten me completely,
reluctantly I hand him two bob
resent it and leave that place.

K.H.

Marianne Larsen
(1951)

SINCE she was twenty, Marianne Larsen has published seven small books of hallucinatory prose poems, reports from a closed universe. From book to book she has opened more and more toward solidarity and human warmth.

Now I Am Gone

Now I am gone
now I am far away
getting thin inside the music

the watch hangs slack from the wrist
I do not see time
it looks like another person
the individual I meet

a big glance in me
growing
away
away in long houses
with hieroglyphs on the walls

away from
its getting out of bed
between façades interior with crowds
between eyes sudden with presence
dream between dream
flesh in air and noise and dust

clothes falling down on
those who wake up
conscious as roles among others
not figures but afraid

P.B.

Sick Women in the Park

thin-legged women
with wigs
when I see you
where did you get your illness
why do you wear a wig of plastic hair
your bird throats
who has taken advantage of you
big-eyed with glasses
you smile when you see me
I am yours
what do you want me to say
when you pass by
you are thinking into the city and past it
smile with a much too broad mouth on the chin
your false teeth have got too big
at night when you sleep painfully
they make you grind your gums
who has taken advantage of you
I'd give you heaven pills if I had any
you should realize everything
you should not walk alone
you should show all the hair you comb out under the wig
        every day
you should not wear a wig
why is the only thing your eyes say when I see them
an anxious excuse for having grown so ugly
you buy the weeklies and the fashion magazines

I know
I have seen you carrying them
you pretend you will buy and try the smart ads of the magazines
you don't even manage to get a new wig
to fasten it properly with little hairpins
there isn't much left to fasten it to
you smile
I can see teeth missing in your artificial mouths
why do you walk restlessly in the parks
you're spreading an odor of still unhealed operations
who has taken advantage of you

                                                                   P.B.

Serial Dream

the lovers will be coming tomorrow
I'll be their
language tomorrow
I am thinking it over and singing
the lovers will be coming tomorrow
who once when I was born
cried
they will be coming tomorrow
as the beach cries for every wave
eyes in a haze
lips touch them
and I hurry to sleep
pictures are walling me in
like forgotten people a lonely journey
the lovers will be coming tomorrow
they think and they come again
there'll be no end to it
and afterwards we are they
and lonely people are spitting out walls
and they see they were standing there before

they are traveling with opened mouths
waiting in opened trains
there are no limits to the whistling of words
no habits for their noise
now the unheard-of ones are coming forth
the lovers will be coming tomorrow

P.B.

Today

today
    I met somebody
            I have known
always
he said
    he had dreamt about
            my isolation
last night
I asked
    how
        you see he said
I dreamt
you had a whole
        lot
        of beautiful people
around you
dreamt
    that your house was alive
          with people
running
in and out
    of the doors
        up and down
          the stairs

talking and smiling
happily
    occupied
        with cutting and sewing
            clothes
in every color
for a party
    to be held
        the same evening
           just think
if the daily isolation
did not exist
    such experiences
        in dreams
would not occur
would not occur
    to be a divine
        compensation
          P.B.

Unknown Person

meeting you face
stained with old water
there is corroding dew inside it
and on the outside are the flowers in the park
on the benches tired people sitting
as though to a folk tune
and waiting
I can see
you have become tear-colored
like brittle glass
in dark draperies
we say
nothing
close our eyes
much too strong blue-light colors
forms fixed thousand-fold
movements in one second's beauty
are crowding to get a look
people abruptly
abandon their waiting
one by one the benches are free
twilight sifts
your face into mine
it happens without leaving scratches and wounds
it happens
quietly laughing

                                    P.B.

Anonymous

as for the words
find their tunes
to prove their spirits
as for the dreams
find their movements
to prove their actions
sing my love and dance
I'll be watching
till you cannot stop
anymore
just go on

Anonymous

I want to imagine
with my mouth
the invisible
black
of your hearts and thoughts
to reread
the transparent goals
of your movements' tomorrows
to meet you again
and unmystify
your intentions with mine

Seven-year-old Girls

I can hear them laughing
remember them playing
sense them smelling
they walk around reading
in a field of daisies
with little ridges
their lips quiver
there are no blind roads and leaves of grass
no blind posts and fences they bump against
no unshakeable electrified little plants
and air and trees and fire
are not turned into crashed airplanes or smashed
cars
in the field where they walk
infernal scoured machine sound has disappeared
panic consciousnesses do not function
dissolved words have sunk into oblivion
the codes of silence do not set the stage for scared cries
in the daisy field are their colors
figures on strong legs
walk as a continuous smiling
growing clarity
fitting
with unlimited confidence
into the manifold hollows and clouds and shades of the sky
in the white and yellow green and blue metamorphoses
of the grass

                                                        P.B.

Acknowledgments

Ove Abildgaard

Terndive (Ternedyk)	*Og Lises hånd i min* 1972
Winter Dream (Vinterdrøm)	*Og Lises hånd i min* 1972
12 Eggs (12 æg)	*Og Lises hånd i min* 1972
Jørgen (Jørgen)	*Og Lises hånd i min* 1972

Benny Andersen

This Uncertainty (Denne uvished)	*Det sidste øh* 1969
Goodness (Godhed)	*Den indre bowlerhat* 1964
M (M)	*Portrætgalleri* 1966
Photographs (Fotografierne)	*Den musikalske ål* 1960
Time (Tiden)	*Her i reservatet* 1971
Life Is Narrow and High (Livet er smalt og højt)	*Personlige papirer* 1974
Earthworm (Regnorm)	*Det sidste øh* 1969
High and Dry (På det tørre)	*Kamera med køkkenadgang* 1962
Melancholy (Melankoli)	*Personlige papirer* 1974
A Hole in the Earth (Et hul i jorden)	*Personlige papirer* 1974

All these poems copyright © 1975 Princeton University Press

Thorkild Bjørnvig

The Ballad of the Great Eastern (Balladen om Great Eastern)	*Figur og ild* 1959
Dysphorial Obituary (Pinlig nekrolog)	*Vibrationer* 1966

Poul Borum

A Green Shed (Et grønt skur)	*Livslinier* 1962
A Train Is Passing (Et tog kører forbi)	*Livslinier* 1962
Pictures from Reality (Billeder fra virkeligheden)	*Dagslys* 1966

331

Against a Wall (Mod en mur)   Dagslys 1966
The Black Picture (Det sorte billede)   Kendsgerninger 1968
The House (Huset)   Den brændende by 1971
While the House Is Burning (Mens huset   I live 1972
   brænder)
Madrigal (Madrigal)   I live 1972
A Fierce Desire (Et hårdt begær)   Denne bog er en drøm 1973
Your Lips, Your Tongue (Dine læber,   Sang til dagens glæde 1974
   din tunge)

Jørgen Gustava Brandt
Sound of the Bell (Klokkes lyd)   Ateliers 1967
Come Aboard (Kom ombord)   Mit hjerte i København 1975
My Element (Mit es)   Der er æg i mit skæg 1966
Night Hour of Suchness (Nattetime af   Der er æg i mit skæg 1966
   sådanhed)
You (Dig)   Ateliers 1967
The House in Copenhagen (Huset i   Fragment af imorgen 1960
   byen)
Patience (Tålmod)   I den høje evighed lød et bil-
   horn 1970
Out of Nothing You Come Walking (Ud   Ateliers 1967
   af intet kommer du gående)
Evident (Åbenbar)   De nødstedte djævle de er de
   værste 1972
It Is the Bird in the Tree (Det er fuglen   Der er æg i mit skæg 1966
   i træet)

Cecil Bødker
Self-portrait (Selvportræt)   Luseblomster 1955
The Companion (Følgesvenden)   Anadyomene 1959
June Night (Juninat)   Anadyomene 1959
   The American Scandinavian Re-
   view June 1974
Under the Sign of the Ram (I væd-   I vædderens tegn 1968
   derens tegn)
Calendar (Kalender)   I vædderens tegn 1968

Inger Christensen
Leaning Tenderly against the Night   Lys 1962
   (Læner mig ømt mod natten)

What Is My Dead Cracked Body (Hvad er min døde sprukne krop) — *Lys* 1962 / *Lines Review* No. 46

In the Wild Mountain Solitude (I bjergenes vilde ensomhed) — *Lys* 1962

Sorrow (Sorg) — *Lys* 1962 / *Lines Review* No. 46

From: "It" (Fra: Det) — *Det* 1969

Sophus Claussen

In an Orchard (I en Frugthave) — *Pilefløjter* 1899

Anadyomene (Anadyomene) — *Danske Vers* 1912

Look, I Met in a Street (Se, jeg mødte paa en Gade) — *Danske Vers* 1912

Heroica (Heroica) — *Heroica* 1925

The Flowing out into Infinity (Udløbet i Uendeligheden) — *Hvededynger* 1930

Robert Corydon

Sea Poem (Havdigt) — *Landskab med huse* 1953

Nettles (Nælder) — *Landskab med huse* 1953

Shout between Two Boats at Sea (Raab mellem to baade paa havet) — *Landskab med huse* 1953

Chinese Brush (Kinesisk pensel) — *Skrænten mod havet* 1955

The Sign (Tegnet) — *Krybet og sommerfuglen* 1958

Spacecraft R101 (Luftskib R101) — *Cyklisten* 1970

Ocean Bridle (Havbidsel) — *Ord til havet* 1968

Tove Ditlevsen

Sunday (Søndag) — *Den hemmelige rude* 1961

Divorce 1* (Skilsmisse 1) — *De voksne* 1969

You Who Someone (Du som ingen) — *Det runde værelse* 1973

The Round Room (Det runde værelse) — *Det runde værelse* 1973

Divorce 3* (Skilsmisse 3) — *De voksne* 1969

Self-portrait 1* (Selvportræt 1) — *De voksne* 1969

Self-portrait 4* (Selvportræt 4) — *De voksne* 1969

* Copyright © 1976 Ann Freeman

Otto Gelsted

Carriage Ride (Køretur) — *Jomfru Gloriant* 1923

The Show Boat (Reklameskibet) — *Jomfru Gloriant* 1923

Per Højholt

November (November)	*Poetens hoved* 1963
M/S Nelly in Countersound (M/S Nelly i modlyd)	*Poetens hoved* 1963
Outside (Udenfor)	*Min hånd* 66 1966
So and so many Larks (Så og så mange lærker)	*Min hånd* 66 1966
A 5-pinnate Leaf (Et femfliget blad)	*The Wormwood Review* No. 46 *Min hånd* 66 1966
The Poet H (Poeten H)	*Min hånd* 66 1966
Frosty Night (Frostnat)	*Min hånd* 66 1966
Turbo 4 (Turbo 4)	*Turbo* 1968

Johannes V. Jensen

At Lunch (Ved Frokosten)	*Digte* 1906
At Memphis Station (Paa Memphis Station)	*Digte* 1906

Frank Jæger

Sunday in September (Søndag i september)	*Dydige digte* 1948
To a Sensitive Girl Friend (Til en følsom veninde)	*Dydige digte* 1948
The Afternoon of the Faun in the Park (Faunens eftermiddag i parken)	*Morgenens trompet* 1949
Small Sun (Liden sol)	*Tyren* 1953
But in September (Men i september)	*Tyren* 1953
Lover (Elsker)	*Havkarlens sange* 1956
Sidenius in Esbjerg (Sidenius i Esbjerg)	*Cinna* 1959
Children Sing like This (Saadan synger børn)	*Idylia* 1967

Per Kirkeby

From: Explanations of Pictures	*Billedforklaringer* 1968
From: Jüngling auf der Wanderschaft	*Jüngling auf der Wanderschaft* 1970
From: 2 Poems	*2 digte* 1973

Erik Knudsen

My Lundbye Ecstasy (Min Lundbyerus)	*Dobbelte dage* 1945
The Flower and the Sword (Blomsten og sværdet)	*Blomsten og sværdet* 1949

Non Scholae (Non scholæ)
The Representatives (Repræsentanterne)
Bourgeois all at Sea (Bourgeois i vildrede)

Sensation og stilhed 1958
Babylon marcherer 1970
Babylon marcherer 1970

Tom Kristensen

The Execution (Henrettelsen)
Grass (Græs)
Fear (Angst)
It's Knud Who Is Dead (Det er Knud, som er død)

Paafuglefjeren 1922
Verdslige Sange 1927
Hærværk 1930
Mod den yderste Rand 1936

Sten Kaalø

For Ever (For Ever)
You Sit out there, Peeing (Der ude sidder du og tisser)
Run (Løbetur)
Recollection (Erindring)

Til folk i byen 1971
Sidste forår 1973

Sidste forår 1973
Sidste forår 1973

Paul la Cour

The Unforeseen (Det Uforudsete)
She Could not Fall (Hun kunne ikke falde)
The Tree (Træet)
Threshold (Tærskel)
Peloponnesian Nights (Peloponnesiske aftner)
Faint Horn-sound of Summer (Sommerens bløde hornlyd)

Levende vande 1946
Mellem bark og ved 1950

Mellem bark og ved 1950
Mellem bark og ved 1950
Efterladte digte 1957

Efterladte digte 1957

Marianne Larsen

Now I Am Gone (Nu er jeg borte)
Sick Women in the Park (De syge koner i parken)
Serial Dream (Seriel drøm)
Today (I dag)
Unknown Person (Ukendt person)
Anonymous I, II (Anonym I, II)
Seven-year-old Girls (Syvårspiger)

Overstregslyd 1972
Ravage 1973

Ravage 1973
Billedtekster 1974
Billedtekster 1974
Cinderella 1974
Cinderella 1974

Acknowledgments 337

Peter Laugesen

Manuscript 4th Version (Manuskript fjerde version) — *Landskab* 1967

November Piece (Novemberstykke) — *Landskab* 1967

From: Writing — *Skrift* 1968

From: Catatonia — *Katatonien* 1970

From: It Is only a Paper Moon — *Det er kun en måne af papir* 1973

From: I Can Hear You Singing — *Jeg kan høre dig synge* 1973

From: Divine Innocence — *Guds ord fra landet* 1974

Jørgen Leth

My Vietnam Poem (Mit Vietnamdigt) — *Lykken i Ingenmandsland* 1967

There Is Always Music through the Walls (Der er altid musik gennem væggene) — *Glatte hårdtpumpede puder* 1969

Tales, Number 10 (Eventyret, No. 10) — *Eventyret om den sædvanlige udsigt* 1971

Tales, Number 15 (Eventyret, No. 15) — *Eventyret om den sædvanlige udsigt* 1971

Hulda Lütken

The Moon Mother (Maanemoderen) — *Klode i drift* 1951

Ivan Malinovski

Love Poem (Kærlighedsdigt I-II) — *Galgenfrist* 1958 / *Lines Review* No. 46

The Petrol Heart (Benzinhjertet) — *Åbne digte* 1963

Demonstration (Demonstration) — *Åbne digte* 1963

Critique of the Way of the World (Kritik af verdens gang) — *Kritik af tavsheden* 1974

Critique of Distraction (Kritik af distraktionen) — *Kritik af tavsheden* 1974

Critique of Myself (Kritik af mig selv) — *Kritik af tavsheden* 1974

Critique of the Child Slayers (Kritik af børnenes banemænd) — *Kritik af tavsheden* 1974

Critique of Freedom (Kritik af friheden) — *Kritik af tavsheden* 1974

Critique of Reason (Kritik af fornuften) — *Kritik af tavsheden* 1974

Critique of Long-suffering (Kritik af langmodigheden) — *Kritik af tavsheden* 1974

338   CONTEMPORARY DANISH POETRY

Critique of Silence (Kritik af tavsheden)   Kritik af tavsheden 1974
Critique of Defeatism (Kritik af de-   Kritik af tavsheden 1974
faitismen)

Tove Meyer
In a Garden back Home (I en have   Drømte digte 1952
derhjemme)

Gustaf Munch-Petersen
The Land Below (det underste land)   det underste land 1933
At the Bottom   Samlede skrifter II 1967
The Special Miracle   Samlede skrifter II 1967
Portrait   Samlede skrifter II 1967
A Little Song   Samlede skrifter II 1967
Song of the Council   Samlede skrifter II 1967
The Certainty   Samlede skrifter II 1967
Etching (rids)   19 digte 1937
Fishing Hamlet (fiskerleje)   19 digte 1937
Winter (vinter)   19 digte 1937
March (marts)   19 digte 1937

Jørgen Nash
Song of Silence (Stilhedens sang)   Salvi Dylvo 1945
Let Us Sing of the Paradise Earth (Lad   Vredens sange 1951
os synge om paradiset jorden)
Dreams Come True Sometimes   Det naturlige smil 1965
World Youth   I denne transistorsommer 1967
Bird Song (illustrated by Asger Jorn)   Stavrim og sonetter 1960
Some People Don't Like Bacon   Sweden and their immigrants
    1975

Hans-Jørgen Nielsen
Mobiles. Variations on the Snow, 1, 2, 5   Verdens/billeder, Udvalgte
(Mobiler. Varitioner over sneen, 1, 2, 5)   stykker 1972
The Body, A Burning Singing-machine   Verdens/billeder, Udvalgte
(Kroppen, den brændende sangmas-   stykker 1972
kine)

Acknowledgments 339

A Few Lines and a Dog (Nogle linier og en hund) From: Figures Moved in Their Images. Not only Her. (Fra: Figurerne bevæget i deres billeder. Ikke blot hende)
A Picture Somewhere in Language (Et billede et sted i sproget)
On the Verge of Poetry (Digt)

Verdens/billeder, Udvalgte stykker 1972
Verdens/billeder, Udvalgte stykker 1972
Verdens/billeder, Udvalgte stykker 1972
Verdens/billeder, Udvalgte stykker 1972

Lean Nielsen

Kurt's Story (Beretningen om Kurt)
Brothers Meet (Brødre mødes)

Egne digte 1973
Egne digte 1973

Morten Nielsen

We're Sending Dance Music at Night (Vi sender dansemusik om natten)
Announcement of a Defeat (Meddelelse om et nederlag)
I See Tonight (Jeg ser nu i nat)
We Couldn't Stay away from Each Other (Vi kunne ikke blive fra hinanden)
They Are Playing Ball on the Road (De spiller bold på vejen)

Krigere uden Vaaben 1943
Krigere uden Vaaben 1943
Efterladte digte 1945
Efterladte digte 1945
Efterladte digte 1945

Henrik Nordbrandt

Disconnection (Afbrydelse)

Stairsong (Trappesang)

German Soldiers' Graves (Tyske soldatergrave)

To a Death Mask (Til en dødsmaske)

When a Person Dies (Når et menneske dør)

Anaesthesia (Narkose)

Digte 1966
Lines Review No. 46
Digte 1966
Lines Review No. 46
Miniaturer 1967
Prism International Fall 1972
Lines Review No. 46
Syvsoverne 1969
Prism International Fall 1972
Lines Review No. 46
Omgivelser 1972
Mundus Artium (not yet published)
Omgivelser 1972

340   CONTEMPORARY DANISH POETRY

Baklava (Baklava)

Byzantium (Byzantium)
In an Asian Village (I en asiatisk
landsby)
A Funeral Portrait (Et gravportræt)
Civil War (Borgerkrig)

Opbrud og ankomster 1974
The Minnesota Review Spring
1975
Opbrud og ankomster 1974
Omgivelser 1972

Opbrud og ankomster 1974
Opbrud og ankomster 1974

Nis Petersen

Spring at Mariager Fjord (Forår ved
Mariager Fjord)
Two Little Old Widows Playing Duet
(To små gamle damer spiller firhændigt)
Elegy 1940 (Elegi 1940)

Nattens Pibere 1926

Stykgods 1940

Stykgods 1940

Bundgård Povlsen

Month of August Poem (Augustmåneds-
digt)
Love Poem (Kærlighedsdigt)
Lizard (Firben)
My Black Windows Shining Miles away
in the Night (Mine sorte vinduer lyser
milevidt i natten)
The Blue Coffee Pot (Den blå kaffe-
kande)
Patience among Trees (Tålmod mellem
træer)
A Superannuated Romantic (En afdanket
romantiker)

Mur og rum 1962

Spor 1964
Spor 1964
Flammekrebsen 1971

Flammekrebsen 1971

Flammekrebsen 1971

Dag/lig/dag 1974

Halfdan Rasmussen

Sardine (Sardin)
Something about Heroes (Noget om
helte)
Old Johnson the Letterbox-painter (No-
get om relative glæder)
Snowman Frost and Lady Thaw (Sne-
mand Frost og frøken Tø)

Med solen i ryggen 1963
Tosserier 1955

Tosserier 1956

Kaspar Himmelspjæt 1955

Klaus Rifbjerg

Birth (Fødsel)

Medieval Morning (Middelaldermorgen)
Zeus in That Mood (Zeus i det humør)
Byron and Company (Byron & Co.)
Spring (Forår)
Afternoon (Eftermiddag)

Under vejr med mig selv 1956
The Scottish International September, 1973
Konfrontation 1960
Mytologi 1970
Mytologi 1970
Scener fra det daglige liv 1973
25 desperate digte 1974

Ole Sarvig

My Sorrow (Min sorg)
Pale Morning (Bleg morgen)
Walk (Vandring)
Skylights (Tagruder)
Thought-stillness (Tankestille)
The Moon's Day (Månens dag)
Christ in the Grain Fields (Kristus i kornet)
Thistles (Tidsler)
Overlooking the Cemetery (Over for kirkegården)
R⁴ (R⁴)

Jeghuset 1944
Jeghuset 1944
Jeghuset 1944
Jeghuset 1944
Jeghuset 1944
Jeghuset 1944
Jeghuset 1944

I forstaden 1966
I forstaden 1966

I forstaden 1966

Jens August Schade

The Heavenly Sun (Den himmelske sol)
Changed Eyes (Forandrede øjne)
Woman (Kvinde)
Equinox (Solhverv)
My Young Love (Min unge elskede)
The Wonderful Vase (Den vidunderlige vase)
Nocturnal Ride (Natlig køretur)
Snow (Sne)
I Love You (Jeg elsker dig)
The Bureau (Chatollet)
At the Movies (I biografen)
A Strawberry (Et jordbær)

Den levende violin 1926
Den levende violin 1926
Den levende violin 1926
Den levende violin 1926
Den levende violin 1926
Hjerte-bogen 1930

Kærlighed og kildevand 1936
Kællingedigte 1944
Kællingedigte 1944
Jordens største lykke 1949
Helvede opløser dig 1953
Schades højsang 1958

Jørgen Sonne

It Is You (Det er dig)

Krese, rhapsodi af digte 1963

The Shepherds' Adoration (Hyrdernes tilbedelse)   *Italiensk suite* 1954
The Fold-out Men (Foldemændene)   *Krese, rhapsodi af digte* 1963
Bird in Mountains (Fugl i bjerge)   *Italiensk suite* 1954

Vagn Steen

I Am no Shower (Jeg er ingen)   *Jeg er ingen* 1967
Technically It Is Possible (Teknisk er det muligt)   *privattryk* 1962
Mirror Mirror on the Wall (Lille spejl)   *Digte?* 1964
$a$capitalistic$society$ (%et%kapitalistisk%samfund%)   *Teknisk er det muligt* 1967

Lise Sørensen

Hold My Hand (Hold mig i hånden)   *Epistler* 1966
In the Dark (I mørket)   *Tro dine øjne* 1973
Boy's Life (Drengeliv)   *Tro dine øjne* 1973
Our Don John (Vor Don Johan)   *Tro dine øjne* 1973
Previously Unpublished (Hidtil utrykt)   *Tro dine øjne* 1973
In a White Kayak (I en hvid kajak)   *Tro dine øjne* 1973

Dan Turèll

From: Karma Cowboy Theme Song   *Karma Cowboy* 1974
From: Song for Blake   *Karma Cowboy* 1974
Canto XXXVII   *Another Draft of Space Cantos* 1974
Canto XLVI   *Another Draft of Space Cantos* 1974

Ole Wivel

The Cologne Cathedral (Domkirken i Køln)   *Nike* 1958
Holy Andrew's Barrow (Hellig Anders høj)   *Gravskrifter* 1970
The Repentant Magdalene of the Roadside (Landevejens bodfærdige Magdalene)   *Gravskrifter* 1970

Stenild Cemetery (Stenild kirkegaard)   *Gravskrifter* 1970
To Poul Winther (Til Poul Winther)   *Gravskrifter* 1970

Johannes Wulff

The Friend Is Dead (Vennen er død)   *Jeg tror min sandten at jeg lever* 1970

Ecstasy of the Flesh (I kødets ekstase)   *Jeg tror min sandten at jeg lever* 1970